Does God Care If I Can't Pay My Bills?

DOES GOD CARE IF I CAN'T PAY MY BILLS?

Comfort and Encouragement for Tough Times

LINDA K. TAYLOR

Tyndale House Publishers, Inc.
WHEATON, ILLINOIS

All Scripture quotations, unless otherwise indicated, are taken from the *Holy Bible,* New International Version®. Copyright © 1973, 1978, 1984 by International Bible Society. Used by permission of Zondervan Publishing House. All rights reserved. The "NIV" and "New International Version" trademarks are registered in the United States Patent and Trademark Office by International Bible Society. Use of either trademark requires permission of International Bible Society.

Scripture verses marked TLB are taken from *The Living Bible,* copyright © 1971 owned by assignment by KNT Charitable Trust. All rights reserved.

Scripture quotations marked NRSV are taken from the New Revised Standard Version of the Bible, copyrighted, 1989 by the Division of Christian Education of the National Council of the Churches of Christ in the United States of America, and are used by permission. All rights reserved.

Scripture quotations marked NKJV are taken from The New King James Version. Copyright © 1979, 1980, 1982, Thomas Nelson Inc., Publishers.

Library of Congress Cataloging-in-Publication Data

Taylor, Linda Chaffee, date
    Does God care if I can't pay my bills? : comfort and encouragement
for tough times / Linda K. Taylor.
        p.   cm.
    Includes bibliographical references and index.
    ISBN 0-8423-1637-X (alk. paper)
    1. Trust in God.   2.   Peace of mind—Religious life—Christianity.
3. Finance, Personal—Religious life—Christianity.   I. Title.
BV4637.T38   1995
248.8′6—dc20   95-8009

Printed in the United States of America

01   00   99   98   97   96   95
 7   6   5   4   3   2   1

To Tom
husband and friend

TABLE OF CONTENTS

Preface ix
1 PAIN 1
Some real-life scenarios
2 PERSPECTIVE 9
Is my glass half full or half empty?
3 PRAYER 21
Is it OK to pray about money?
4 PLAN 41
Failing to plan is the same as planning to fail
5 PRIORITIES 61
Wealth is relative—now what I need is a rich relative!
6 PRIDE 77
A head held high can look up to God
7 PATIENCE 89
Why don't I get any miracles?
8 PEACE 99
An island of peace in a sea of trouble
Notes 115
Index 117

PREFACE

This book is intended to be your life preserver while you try to stay afloat during your particular financial crisis. Each person's crisis is different. If it is causing you pain, it *is* a crisis for you, whether or not it is better or worse than anyone else's. You've fallen off the "financial ship," and you need help to keep from drowning and to stay clear of the sharks.

What I want you to get from this book is reassurance that, even if your prayers for relief seem to be falling on deaf ears, God still cares. I want you to keep your faith, even if you lose everything else.

Rest assured, I am not giving trite answers from an "I've been through it, and now we're fine, so it will all work out for you too" perspective. I am daily challenged to put into practice what I'm learning and writing to you. My husband and I continue to trust God for guidance in some difficult days.

I'm trying to find the light at the end of the tunnel myself. At times I'm certain that, when it comes to financial struggles, we have been God's dartboard. At times I've gotten to the point of deciding that God truly doesn't care—even though, deep down, I know he does.

Journey with me. We may see the light in a matter of days or weeks. Maybe when we finally glimpse it, it will be the light of heaven. But God is molding us, teaching us about what really matters. That is the lesson we really need to learn.

CHAPTER 1
PAIN
Some real-life scenarios

Those who do not feel pain seldom think that it is felt.
SAMUEL JOHNSON

Lloyd and Karen Wright (not their real names) have taken a beating financially. A few years ago, with high hopes and wild dreams, they bought a fixer-upper house, started their own construction business, and started their family. Five years later, their fixer-upper has changed little, for all their money and time have gone into the business and their children. With more than fifty thousand dollars owed to them by builders who went bankrupt, homeowners who bounced checks, "friends" who never paid for work done, and contractors who simply dealt dishonestly with them, Lloyd and Karen are battling to live month to month. Sure, all the outstanding money is supposedly being collected by lawyers, but there is little real hope of ever getting justice. They're trying to keep up, trying to pay their bills, but it gets tougher every month as new crises arise on top of the old ones. Lloyd and Karen wonder if they'll ever be able to stop worrying about money.

Lloyd and Karen have a crisis. They have been unjustly treated. Even the legal system affirms that much, despite the fact that it is in no hurry to help them. They have

1

purchased and used materials without getting reimbursed for them—and the suppliers are demanding payment. The regular bills keep adding up. New crises continue to occur—the truck breaks down, the kids get sick. The Wrights sincerely want to pay their bills, but the money just isn't there to do it. They are in pain—hurt and hopeless. They have been able to work out payment plans with all their creditors, and this has stopped the harassing phone calls . . . at least for this month. But what about next month? Will they ever be able to pay off their debts when new crises keep cropping up? They couldn't afford to buy Christmas presents for their kids (thank goodness for relatives), and there will be no vacations or music lessons or other extras until this round of debt is paid. Lloyd and Karen are slowly but surely losing hope—and sadly, their faith is dying too. It seems that God doesn't care.

◆ ◆ ◆

Sam Peterson had been climbing the ladder at corporate headquarters. At the top rung of the middle-management ladder, he was ready to step into a vice presidency. But the company was recently bought out, and Sam was abruptly advised that he was no longer needed. His triple-figure income vanished. Sam has two mortgages on his high-class house in the suburbs, multiple credit-card accounts charged to the maximum, loans for two brand-new cars, a fur on layaway for his wife for their anniversary, and large pledges to his church and various missionaries that he feels obliged to honor. Sam has always been very generous, but he realizes that he now has a serious problem. The bills will keep coming, but the large paychecks won't, at least for a while.

Sam has a crisis. He seemed to have the golden touch; money was always there for anything he or his family needed or wanted. And Sam was one of the rare breed who don't let their money control them. He was generous and willing to give to others in need. But suddenly the golden touch lost its magic; there would be no more big paychecks. This is new for Sam, and he is in pain because of the choices he must make. The bills for the house, the credit cards, the cars, the fur, and the generous pledges are still there, but Sam doesn't have enough money to pay for them. Sam overextended himself, and now he's being called upon to pay up. Sam feels trapped and hopeless. And he feels ashamed.

◆ ◆ ◆

Mitch and Carol Jones have always been a little free with their spending. And why not? For years, Mitch had his own remodeling business; Carol had a high-paying midmanagement computer job with great benefits. Carol carried their health insurance through her company, so everything was always covered—from minor doctor's appointments to dental work to their minor surgeries. Then Carol got pregnant and decided to stay home with the baby. Mitch and Carol procrastinated about getting their own health insurance after Carol left her job. Then one day, Mitch fell off a ladder and broke his back. Surgery and rehabilitation have been extremely costly, and Mitch has been warned not to work at his previous job or he may become permanently disabled. Now neither Mitch nor Carol has a job, and their medical bills are in the tens of thousands of dollars.

Mitch and Carol's marriage is on the verge of ruin. After all the fun they used to have with money, now they worry about simply making ends meet. They're fighting about whether Carol should go back to work and who would watch the baby or whether Mitch should go on working and risk further injury. They can't sleep because they're so worried about their house payments, their school loans, their credit-card bills, and Mitch's truck loan, not to mention the thousands of dollars owed to the neurosurgeon, the hospital, the anesthesiologist, the pathologists, the rehabilitation specialists, and on and on. They are in pain and are taking it out on each other. They feel helpless and hopeless.

♦ ♦ ♦

After thirty-two years at the factory, Harry Mitchell was ready to retire next year. He's given his whole life to this place and watched it grow from a family-owned business to a multi-million-dollar company. Harry has worked hard all his life, looking forward to the day when he and his wife could retire on his pension, enjoy traveling, and give some special gifts to his kids and their families. But decisions were recently made in the executive offices that dashed Harry's plans to pieces. Hundreds of workers have been laid off, most of them older ones with the high pensions. The company chose to pay them as little as legally possible to help alleviate its own financial bind. Harry walked away with a few dollars of severance pay, knowing the top executives have multimillion-dollar salaries. Now Harry must put aside his dreams for the reality of figuring out a way to pay his monthly bills.

Harry is downright mad. He's in a crisis—an unjust crisis as far as he's concerned. The company made a deliberate choice to cut the most loyal long-term employees. It was a low blow. Harry hadn't saved a whole lot over the years; he never really made that much to begin with. He helped his kids through college and depended on his pension for his retirement. Harry is in pain over the injustice of his thousand-dollar-suit-clad bosses. They have left him with a bleak future, and Harry can't do anything about it. Harry is mad, and he's without hope.

◆ ◆ ◆

Marion Andrews has been through some difficult days. Her son's death in a car accident changed her life forever. Her husband, Chuck, was never able to get over it, and grew more and more depressed. Among other things, he began to buy things on credit to try to assuage the depression, but he could never pull through. Deeply disturbed, Chuck finally took his own life. Marion had tried to keep her faith strong, even while Chuck floundered, but this time her pain was more than she could bear. Then she found out that Chuck's life-insurance policy would not pay in the case of suicide. Marion is now being hounded for all of the bills because she was a cosigner on all of them—the new truck, the new boat, the credit cards. Marion hasn't worked for years and never really even knew anything about the household finances because Chuck handled them all. She must face not only another tragedy but the reality of Chuck's unpaid debts, for which she is responsible.

Marion's pain is immeasurable. She's still grieving over her son's death, and now she carries the additional burden of her husband's suicide. She wonders if she was somehow at fault; she wonders why God would allow her to face two such horrible tragedies. She is beginning to feel that God has left her. She looks at their finances on the computer and tries to figure out where their money was going and how she is going to make ends meet now that she is all alone.

◆ ◆ ◆

Ruth Hoover's husband came home a few weeks ago and told her he had found another woman and would be leaving that night. Ruth, still in shock, went to the bank the next day, only to discover that her husband had emptied all their checking and savings accounts. Now he is fighting her at every turn, apparently attempting to leave her and the children completely destitute. Ruth can't believe this is happening.

Ruth's pain is deep. The man she loved and trusted for so many years has betrayed that trust and now seems to delight in causing her as much trouble—financial and otherwise—as he can. She has gotten a kind lawyer to work at a reasonable rate and take payments. He has helped her work out some of the financial arrangements, but she still has basic living expenses and mounting legal expenses to cover.

◆ ◆ ◆

Each of these scenarios is based on a true story, but the names and details have been changed for privacy's sake. After reading each of them, what common elements do you see? There are at least four:

1. Each is a crisis.
2. Each crisis includes bills that need to be paid when there is no money to pay them.
3. Each crisis is causing pain.
4. Each crisis seems to have no solution.

Since you're reading this book, you are probably in a financial crisis too, or you know someone who is. Your personal story may be similar to one of these scenarios or totally different. But chances are that the same four basic elements of financial crisis are part of your situation.

Something has happened that has thrown your security, your budget, your daily routine, or your hopes and dreams to the wind. Perhaps your self-esteem has also disappeared. Maybe you've taken on a load of guilt in addition to the load of overdue bills. You truly care about honoring your debts and want to pay them, but circumstances have spun out of your control, and you just can't do it.

Unfortunately, a financial crisis can cause a Christian's faith to become shaky. You may wonder how God could allow this to happen, why he doesn't bring relief, why he doesn't bring justice, why he seems so deaf to your pleas. You can't sleep; you're overwhelmed with worry; you're afraid of losing everything you've worked for.

I have been there. I am still not completely out of the woods. I am writing this book for you, my friend, because you need lots of encouragement to get through each day, to know that life is still worth living, to know that there is light at the end of the tunnel.

Since every crisis is unique, I cannot presume to deal with every aspect of your crisis. While all financial crises share the four common elements we identified, each one—including yours—also has specific circumstances that create special needs. In the examples we looked at, Lloyd and Karen need legal advice, Sam needs help learning how to live in a lower income bracket, and both Marion and Ruth probably need Christian counseling (from a pastor or an agency rather than anything costly) to help them deal with their grief. You, too, may need expert advice or guidance in order to deal with certain aspects of your situation. While I will focus on helping you through the financial crisis, I may be dealing with only a symptom of a deeper problem. As helpful as I hope that will be to you, I pray that you will be able to find complete healing where it is needed in other areas of your life.

In this book I want to focus on the heaviness of your financial burden and help you get a handle on it from several specific directions:

- In chapter 2 we'll look at keeping your *perspective* on life, even when the bills seem overwhelming.
- Chapter 3 discusses *prayer*. You can pray about money and about your financial crisis. God does hear and care, whether he seems to answer or not.
- Chapter 4 offers practical help you can start using right away: a *plan* to use in paying off your bills. The monthly grind of matching paycheck to bills can be reduced to a system with which you can keep everyone happy and begin to see results.
- Chapter 5 will help you set *priorities* as you consider various ways to work through your crisis.
- In chapter 6 we'll talk about *pride* and its effect on your crisis. I want to help you see that you can ask for help, you can accept help when it is offered, and you should seek counsel regarding your crisis.
- Chapter 7 helps you work on your *patience* so that you don't make comparisons between your situation and someone else's.
- Chapter 8 looks at how you can find *peace* in the middle of your crisis.

Let's begin our journey. There *is* light at the end of the tunnel.

CHAPTER 2
PERSPECTIVE
Is my glass half full or half empty?

There is no education like adversity.
BENJAMIN DISRAELI

A s I said in the introduction, this book is intended to be a life preserver to keep you afloat during your particular financial crisis. But a life preserver can't do much good if you don't use it.

Picture the scenario: You've fallen off the "financial ship" and are frantically splashing in the ocean, seeking something to keep you afloat. Someone throws you a life jacket. But if you keep splashing in fear, you won't be able to grab the life jacket, much less put it on.

What must you do? Relax, take a breath, tread water, and calmly grab the life jacket.

Relaxing, taking a deep breath, and treading water during your financial crisis means *getting a proper perspective*. You can't begin to get help or to help yourself until you put the crisis in perspective.

Don't get me wrong. I'm not belittling your crisis. It *is* a crisis. But money problems are insidious and overwhelming, causing us to lose perspective on the problem as it relates to other areas of life.

All the people in the crises described in chapter 1 might very easily begin to lose that one quality that could keep them

9

from drowning—*perspective.* Each crisis is large, as is yours, but it need not loom into gargantuan proportions that make you unable to function during the day and unable to sleep at night. So how do we keep it manageable? How do we regain our perspective?

Let's look at four common reactions of people in financial crises. See if you identify with any or all of these examples:

- You pray, but God doesn't seem to hear—so you lose perspective on his care for you.
- You blame or want to blame someone (yourself, your spouse, the unjust person who hurt you, even God)—so you lose perspective on the source of the problem.
- You feel that, while money is the problem, it is also the solution; if only you could get enough money, your problems would be solved—so you lose perspective on the power of money.
- You allow the volume of the crisis to block out everything else in your life—so you lose perspective on what really matters.

Let's examine each of these possible reactions in more detail.

WHY PRAY?

You pray, but God doesn't seem to hear—so you lose perspective on his care for you.

If you're a believer, you have probably been praying from the moment your crisis began. Sometimes even unbelievers are pushed into prayer as they lose all hope. Hopefully, it was your first reaction. However, you've been praying for weeks or even months and seem to have received no answer.

10

You prayed the "pray without doubting" prayer (James 1:6). You decided that God cared and would help you out, and you did not doubt one bit. Certain of God's ultimate help, you pled with him to meet your needs.

Silence.

You prayed the "persistent" prayer (Luke 18:1), turning to God moment by moment; deciding, like the woman in Jesus' parable, not to stop praying until an answer came. You've cried and pled for days, weeks on end.

Silence.

You prayed the specific prayer "in Jesus' name" (John 14:13-14). You looked over your bills and told God exactly the amount you needed to pay them off, or just to meet this month's requirements. You asked God for this amount, knowing that your motivation was pure. You simply want to pay your bills; you're not asking for anything for yourself. You can confidently pray "in Jesus' name" because certainly it is God's will that you meet your obligations.

Silence.

You prayed and claimed a miracle (Mark 9:23). After all, God's business is miracles, right? He certainly has the resources; you were confident that what you wanted was within his will, so you claimed his promises to meet your needs.

Silence.

Then you combined all the prayers into one: a persistent, specific prayer in Jesus' name, claiming a miracle without doubting.

Silence.

Then you started to lose perspective. Maybe God doesn't care at all. Maybe God doesn't really hear prayer. You may even be facing the ultimate doubt: Maybe there isn't a God. All the Sunday school answers don't help you understand God's apparent silence during your crisis.

We will examine prayer during a financial crisis in more detail in chapter 3.

THE "NO FAULT" CLAUSE

You blame or want to blame someone (yourself, your spouse, the unjust person who hurt you, even God)—so you lose perspective on the source of the problem.

Marion and Ruth (from chapter 1) certainly have a good place to put the blame for their situations. Marion's husband left her with all the bills; Ruth's husband is *trying* to give her financial problems. There are spouses who drink or gamble away paychecks, who run up credit cards, who make needless purchases (buying one large item or frittering money away on small items). Some manic-depressive people go out and spend money when they start feeling down—and there's little even the most caring spouse can do to stop it. If you find yourself in a similar situation, your first priority will be to find out exactly what the problem is and face it. Only when it is defined can you begin to work on it. If the problem is severe, counseling may be needed. If alcohol or gambling or manic depression is the problem, seek professional help. There are many books that can help; there are many Christian counselors and organizations that want to help you work through the problem. Find them and try to get the help you need. If your spouse won't admit a problem or won't join you, go anyway—you need the support. And pray, pray, pray.

You may be able to solve the problem by talking through a budget with your spouse that allows you each a certain amount of "mad money" from each paycheck—money that can be spent any way you want. Even a small amount, as little as five dollars, can be helpful. A friend told me she and her husband allow each other twenty dollars every month that doesn't need to be accounted for. She claims, "It works!" and that it helps to relieve the stress. One time, I had five dollars to spend just for myself. I bought some new nail polish and a cup of cappuccino—and I felt like a queen!

If you can do it, try to make solving the crisis a team effort (sometimes the whole family can be enlisted to help). If everyone knows the extent of the problem and works toward a solution (and knows that some of the sacrifices are only temporary), then you have gained communication, extra ideas and resources, and a team spirit. When you've got people on your side, working with you, the crisis seems much easier to bear. Mitch and Carol need to stop casting blame at each other over the crisis they're in and start working together on a solution. They are both creative, bright people—they're wasting energy blaming each other, and they're not coming up with any answers.

The source of your crisis might be outside the family unit, outside your control, like with Lloyd and Karen: They were fine until people cheated them out of deserved money, and that caused their downward spiral. They wanted to blame those who hurt them. You also might have a target for your blame—someone against whom you can claim, "It's all his fault!" Someone about whom you can fantasize all the nasty things you'd like to do to get your own brand of revenge. Someone you hate vehemently . . . someone—

Hold it! Get the picture? Blaming others wastes a lot of energy. Blaming gives too much power to the object of your blame, allowing him or her to consume your thoughts as well as the time and energy you should be spending elsewhere. Ruth, needing to face her unfaithful husband, also needs to avoid wasting precious energy blaming him. While he may be to blame, she needs energy to continue her daily life, to help her kids, to keep her mental health, and to work through the crisis. Don't allow that person so much power over you. Get your perspective back.

Try not to place blame. The source of the problem is not that you married the wrong person—it is sin. Our fallen human nature is, at times, overwhelming even for believers. Don't add destroying your marriage to the crisis you already face. Your situation is different from anyone else's, but don't allow the crisis to take your eyes off the value of your marriage and family. Do whatever it takes to keep your family together—communicate, get counseling, keep praying (even if you're doing it alone), and trust God. God does care about you, your crisis, your spouse, your family.

Maybe God is the one you blame—carefully, tremblingly—but still holding him responsible. Mitch and Carol, after they tire of blaming each other, might try to blame God for causing the crisis—who else? Why would God allow Mitch to fall off a ladder when they hadn't gotten health insurance yet? And if God was going to allow it to happen, why didn't he give them the resources to deal with it? But Mitch and Carol need to remember that while they were caught by surprise, God wasn't. In many ways they don't see and might never know, God *did* go before them, preparing the way and taking care of them.

It's also possible that your financial crisis has caused you to look within yourself. If God is pointing out sin in your life—that may or may not have caused the crisis—that sin needs to be dealt with. However, don't allow yourself to be overwhelmed by guilt (*How could I have done this to my family?* or *How can God ever forgive me of this sin?*). God does not point out our sin so he can stand in heaven and laugh while we squirm. Instead, he calls us lovingly back to his forgiving arms.

Remember, God is concerned about *all* of life—his goal is to help you grow to be more like him. Life is full of difficult situations, not the least of which is paying past-due bills. While God is concerned about those bills, he is more concerned about your becoming more and more like him, no matter what circumstances you face. Your crisis may be part of that growth. Don't blame yourself and shut yourself off from what God has to say to you—that's like blaming yourself for falling into the ocean and saying you shouldn't get into the life jacket because you don't deserve it. When you begin to humbly listen to God's words to you, you will experience peace and growth in the middle of your crisis.

Look your sin in the face and deal with it. If you need professional help, get it. If you need forgiveness from your spouse or someone else, ask for it. If you need to forgive yourself and get on with your life, do it. Keep your perspective.

In order to get perspective on your crisis, remove the word *fault* from your vocabulary. It's not your fault or the fault of your spouse, your employer, your defaulting customers, or God. Good things happen in life; bad things happen; crises happen. Your crisis just happened, and it needs to be handled. If you stop casting blame, you'll have more energy to deal with it.

LOTTO JACKPOTS AND OTHER CRACKPOTS

You feel that, while money is the problem, it is also the solution; if only you could get enough money, your problems would be solved—so you lose perspective on the power of money.

I had a dream one night that Elizabeth Taylor was visiting my trailer (I have never met Elizabeth Taylor, and I don't own a trailer!), and she said to me, "Just tell me how much will take care of the problem" and then wrote me a check.

Wouldn't that be great?

15

Money is powerful; money problems are overwhelming. As you lie awake at night racking your brain to figure out what you can sell, what more work you can do—how you can possibly bring in a few more dollars—you can't help but think that maybe someone will become your benefactor. Maybe some relative you never heard of will die and leave you a cool million.

Maybe if you just play a few times, you can win the lottery.

Maybe if you're just consistent enough, you can be one of those "lucky people" pictured on the Publishers Clearinghouse mailings.

Maybe you're not even dreaming that big. If you could just sell that collection of comics, that old car, that coin, or that piece of art, you'd be in the clear.

You can't stop thinking about it, figuring, hoping against hope.

And you're losing your perspective. Money has become your master. Jesus said, "You cannot serve both God and Money" (Matthew 6:24). The apostle Paul wrote, "For the love of money is a root of all kinds of evil" (1 Timothy 6:10, NKJV).

Money is a cruel and relentless master. Before you read any further in this book, you must come to the realization that money will not solve all your problems. Say it aloud right now:

"MONEY WILL NOT SOLVE ALL MY PROBLEMS."

Say it again with conviction. A check for $50,000 that will pay all your bills will not arrive. You will not win the lottery (so stop playing and wasting your money). You will not win the Publishers Clearinghouse sweepstakes—go ahead, mail back the "certificates" for a while, but when they threaten to dump you unless you buy magazines, dump them. Get your perspective back.

Remember the quote at the beginning of this section:

"There is no education like adversity." You are in process. This crisis is part of the process of your growth. God's only goal in your life is to make you more like himself. He is not interested in making your life easy; he is interested in helping you grow spiritually. When you look to money to solve your problems, you're looking at the wrong master.

This brings us back to prayer. What were you praying for all that time? Money, right? Why? Because you thought money would solve all your problems. Sounded innocent enough, but it was wrong. God wasn't answering your prayer because you asked for the wrong thing. He probably won't make you rich, for he knows the pitfalls of riches.

Turn your prayers around. Pray for yourself—that you'll learn what God wants you to learn. Pray for your spouse, your family, that they too will grow spiritually. Pray for your enemy, the inflicter (bet that's one prayer you *haven't* tried!). Jesus' words are very clear: "Pray for those who *persecute* you! In that way you will be acting as true sons of your Father in heaven" (Matthew 5:44-45, TLB).

Stop looking to the wrong master. Keep your perspective.

HOLDING ON FOR DEAR LIFE

You allow the volume of the crisis to block out everything else in your life—so you lose perspective on what really matters.

If you're like me, your financial crisis keeps you awake at night—causing you to be even more tired and unable to deal with the crisis and keep your perspective. You cry a lot. You're short-tempered with the kids. The bill collectors call and you cry some more. You dread answering the phone and opening the mail. You can't function at times, can't concentrate. You feel out of control, helpless, and hopeless. The crisis is tuning out the rest of your life.

It gets plenty of help. Let's start with those bill collectors, paid to harass you and make you feel like you're either a criminal or a total loser. Believe me, I dealt with plenty of them. We will look at ways to handle bill collectors in chapter 8.

I've kept repeating the need to keep your perspective. What should that perspective be? Perspective is merely your understanding of the facts you face and their relationship. Most days you feel like this:

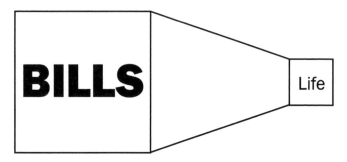

You literally and figuratively make your financial situation "bigger than life."

I suggest an alternative:

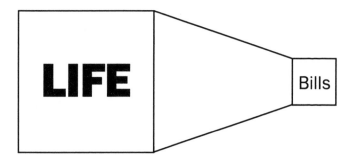

Granted, you cannot pretend the bills aren't there. You *do* have an obligation to pay them. Throwing them in the desk drawer unopened won't make them go away. But ask yourself these questions:

- Does Visa lie awake at night worrying about me?
- Will life as I know it end if I miss this payment?
- What's the worst that can happen?

Now consider these questions:

- My toddler won't be a toddler for long—what have we enjoyed today?
- Am I allowing this problem to erect a wall between me and my spouse or my kids?
- Isn't the weather beautiful today?

Get the picture? Give your child a hug, and go do something free and enjoyable! Don't waste any more precious moments of life in turmoil over a problem you have no power to solve.

THERE WILL ALWAYS BE CRISES

Here's a sobering thought: You'll get through this crisis, but there will be other types of crises—some big, some small. You will always face problems. Will you handle them by being so stressed that you snap at your children and cannot see beyond the problem? Or will you "cast all your cares upon God" and calmly help your child with her homework? Learn the lesson now, and the next crisis will be easier to handle. You'll be in tune with God, and you won't let the crisis overpower you. You'll keep your perspective. You'll know

- that God *does* care about you
- that casting blame only wastes time and energy

- that God—not money—is sovereign and in control
- that what *really* matters are your relationship with God and the blessings that exist right under your nose

What difference will this make? An entire world of difference—you'll get your life back! The crisis may not be over, the problem isn't gone, the phone is still ringing with those nasty creditors on the line, but you've *enjoyed* the day—loving your family, enjoying the weather, playing with the dog, whatever.

Don't let the need for money take those things away. You can catch up on your bills—but you can't catch up on lost time.

Keep your perspective.

CHAPTER 3

PRAYER

Is it OK to pray about money?

Do not pray for easy lives. Pray to be stronger men.
Do not pray for tasks equal to your powers.
Pray for powers equal to your tasks.
PHILLIPS BROOKS

As believers, we've known from our Sunday school days that God hears and answers prayer. But somehow this situation is different. When you realized the financial crisis you were in, your first response might have been a despairing cry to God for help . But you may have wondered, even as you prayed, *Is it OK to pray about money?*

Perhaps days and weeks passed, and nothing seemed to improve—or the situation got even worse. You began to wonder why God was silent. We explored briefly in chapter 2 the possibility that God's apparent silence or refusal to pull you out of your crisis might lead you to doubt your faith, the power of prayer, or even God himself.

Lloyd and Karen (from chapter 1) wonder why God would allow injustice to put them into a crisis. Why would God (or even the law itself) allow people to just refuse to pay and leave them no recourse? Harry, too, feels the sting of injustice as he looks at his meager severance pay after giving so much to the company.

21

Mitch and Carol want to know why God would give them a medical disaster without any help to deal with it. Marion and Ruth wonder the same thing: Why would God allow such bad things to happen and leave them with no help and little hope?

They all are wondering why. They all are praying for help.

God's silence might cause you to do some self-examination—and that can be positive. But what happens if you feel that it was your own mistakes that got you into this crisis? Mitch and Carol might have felt this way as they realized that their own procrastination in getting health insurance put them in their crisis. You too may feel like you *jumped* off the financial ship, and even though you're in danger of drowning, you shouldn't yell for help because it's your own fault.

How are we to pray in the middle of a financial crisis? Can we pray about money? Can we ask God to help us out of a crisis that we got ourselves into?

BACK TO THE BASICS

Before addressing those questions, let's go back to the basics—the who, what, when, where, why, and how of prayer. If you have come into a personal relationship with God through his Son, Jesus Christ, he is your Father; you are his child. Relationships are built by communication. We communicate with our heavenly Father through prayer.

Who is involved in prayer?

In private prayer, it's you and God. You must first have a personal relationship with God in order to pray effectively. You need to have accepted Jesus Christ as your personal Savior and Lord before you can come into God's presence with your prayers. You are praying not to an image, or to the stars, or to some New Age idea of an outside force; you are praying to God himself, the Creator of the universe. When you come before God in prayer, you have his full and undivided attention. You are talking to someone who truly loves you, cares about what is best for you, and has promised to answer you. Prayer is an enormous privilege. God *wants* his people to communicate with him.

You may feel all alone in your crisis. But in prayer, you have the ear of God himself. He wants you to talk to him about everything. He wants you to communicate your needs to him. You and God, or you and your spouse and family and God, can talk together because God promises to listen to his children.

What can you talk about with God?
When and where should you do it?
He wants you to talk with him about anything, and he can be reached from any place at any time. Paul's advice to "pray continually" (1 Thessalonians 5:17) means that God wants every aspect of your life to be enveloped by prayer. Talking with God throughout the day should be as natural as breathing. As you go through your day, you can

- talk to God about how you feel
- ask for his advice as you run into situations that need his guidance and wisdom
- praise him for who he is and what he has done as these thoughts come to mind
- thank him for his blessings as you see and think of them
- confess sins
- intercede on behalf of others
- ask him for help in personal needs

In addition, you should have a regular quiet time set aside for focused prayer. While he was on earth, Jesus was in constant communication with God, yet the Gospels record times when Jesus went away alone to pray. Remember that prayer is communication; that implies both talking and listening. You ask God for help and guidance, but you also need to listen for his answers.

The crisis you're facing is probably intruding into every aspect of your life and overwhelming you. God wants you to turn to him every time the crisis threatens to tear you down. Pray when the worry causes a knot in your stomach; send up a prayer as you open the mail or answer the phone; ask God to help you see the blessings that surround you, and thank him for them; ask for guidance and wisdom; ask for perspective; ask for peace. He wants to help you with your needs. In your quiet times of prayer, talk to God as your best friend and pour out your questions, your fears, your worries, your needs.

The book of 2 Kings tells a wonderful story of King Hezekiah—one of the few God-fearing kings of Judah. Sennacherib, king of the mighty Assyrian empire, swept down toward Jerusalem, defeating everyone in his path. He sent a letter to King Hezekiah saying Hezekiah's God could not help Jerusalem, for no one could stand against Sennacherib. When Hezekiah read the letter, "he went up to the temple of the Lord and spread it out before the Lord. And Hezekiah prayed . . . 'Give ear, O Lord, and hear; open your eyes, O Lord, and see; listen to the words Sennacherib has sent to insult the living God'" (2 Kings 19:14-16). Then Hezekiah prayed for God to deliver Jerusalem. The end of chapter 19 describes God's miraculous deliverance of the city. Hezekiah's humble prayer changed the course of his nation and that of the Assyrian empire.

Your crisis doesn't involve saving a nation, but it does involve a situation that feels as hopeless as an attack by the Assyrian army. Take those hopeless bills and those dunning letters, and place them before God, humbly asking for his help. Then listen for God's answer and guidance.

Why should you pray?

Does prayer really make any difference? If God already knows all your needs, if God already knows the future, what good does it do to pray? Can prayer make things happen or change God's mind? In an article titled "Responding to God in Prayer," Dr. James Boice answers those questions this way:

> If we pray, will things happen that would not happen if we did not pray? The answer is certainly yes. But how does that work? If God has a perfect, sovereign will, how can our prayers have any effect whatsoever? The answer is this: God never accomplishes his purposes without means.
>
> Prayer is one of the means God has appointed by which to accomplish his will. God says, "I'm going to do this, and the means by which I'm going to do it is prayer. I'm going to do it in response to the prayers of my people."
>
> This not only means that God knows what we are going to pray. It also means, in some way our finite minds cannot possibly comprehend, that if we do not pray, the thing will not happen. If we pray according to God's will, which is what we should do, it will happen. . . .
>
> We have a great responsibility in prayer. Prayer is not an empty exercise. It is vital. We have to take those verses at face value; if we don't receive, it's because we don't ask. If we ask according to God's will in the name of Christ, we will receive.[1]

So we pray because God wants us to communicate with him. We pray because we need to stay in contact with our Lord in order to keep a living and growing relationship with him. We pray because, through our prayers, God accomplishes his work in the world.

What does that mean in your crisis? That you *must* pray about it. Regardless of the cause or the magnitude or your feelings, you must pray for help. Then God has a chance to work, and when he does, you give *him* the praise.

How should you pray?

First, you should *pray regularly and persistently.* Jesus was in constant contact with the Father, and he admonished his disciples "that they should always pray and not give up" (Luke 18:1). God wants to hear from you on the good days and the bad days. He wants you to be in communication all the time. When there is a need, he wants you to pray and not give up.

Second, you should *pray truthfully.* When you pray, you are talking to your best friend; there's no point in not telling the whole story or trying to hide anything. God knows you through and through, so your prayers might as well be completely honest. Psalm 139:1-2 says, "O Lord, You have searched me and known me. You know my sitting down and my rising up; You understand my thought afar off" (NKJV). God already knows the amounts of all the bills; he already knows the background of your crisis; he already knows the pain and guilt involved. But tell him anyway. Tell him your true feelings. Let him know how angry or hurt or confused you are. If you doubt that God wants to hear those feelings, read some of the psalms. David, who wrote many of the psalms, poured out hatred, anger, revenge, guilt, sorrow, and confession in his talks with God. You can do the same.

Third, you should *pray confidently.* Hebrews 4:16 calls believers to "come boldly to the throne of grace" (NKJV). When we request an audience with the King, he is always happy to hear us. You have a need. God has the resources. The obvious answer is to take that need to God. Pray, knowing that God hears and will answer. Then leave your burden there.

Hannah is a beautiful example of praying with confidence. Hannah had been unable to have children, and this caused her much pain. She couldn't eat; she cried all the time. Then, on a trip to Shiloh with her husband and his other wife (who had children), she brought her request for a son to God's tabernacle. She prayed, talked to the priest, and "went her way and ate something, and her face was no longer downcast" (1 Samuel 1:18). She brought her seemingly impossible request to God and left it there. She no longer worried or cried; she trusted God and patiently awaited his answer. You, too, can pray with such confidence.

At times your pain is so deep and your burden so heavy that you don't even know what to pray. When you feel that way, kneel quietly before God, and though you may be unable to mouth any words, God hears your heart. Scripture promises, "In the same way, the Spirit helps us in our weakness. We do not know what we ought to pray for, but the Spirit himself intercedes for us with groans that words cannot express. And he who searches our hearts knows the mind of the Spirit, because the Spirit intercedes for the saints in accordance with God's will" (Romans 8:26-27).

GOD ALWAYS ANSWERS

While it seems right that we would pray for a friend's salvation or for the safety of missionaries or for God's guidance of national issues, it somehow seems wrong or selfish to bother God about our financial problems. It's even worse if we know we brought the problem on ourselves: How can we ask God to get us out of a jam that we put ourselves into? And money seems so . . . well, *worldly*. It doesn't have anything to do with salvation or heaven, so is it right to ask God for needed funds?

But if you go to the root of that question, you'll get something like this: Are some prayers insignificant to God? And the answer clearly is no. No request is insignificant; God does not ignore his children any more than a loving parent ignores a child. Whether the request is for a certain kind of cereal or for guidance in setting goals for the future, a parent responds to a child. Whether we are praying about the nation's financial state or praying over our own checkbook, God hears and responds.

God may answer your prayer for money with a resounding yes and allow the money to arrive on schedule. A friend just described her recent dealings with God in a financial crisis: She told God she needed three thousand dollars in two days—otherwise the utilities would be shut off and other commitments would not be met. God provided a job and cash advance that met the need, and he did it in those two days.

God may answer your prayer with a no. But a no doesn't mean he doesn't care. If your toddler asks if he can play in the street, you of course say no. And you say no because you care, not because you don't. The same goes for our heavenly Father. He has a reason for his answer. He knows the outcome; he knows what he wants you to learn. What you asked for might be as dangerous as playing in the street, so God wisely declines the request. Or what you asked for may be wrong—perhaps your motivation or attitude was wrong. Then you need to clear that up with God before you come back to your financial needs. For example, someone might pray to win the lottery, thinking all that money would pay all the bills. The motivation *seems* right (bills will be paid), and the person might even promise to give the rest of the money to the church. But God, who knows the dangers of wealth, usually says no to that request. Whenever there's a no answer, there might be a yes answer in another direction, if you take the time to listen to God's guidance.

God may answer your prayer with a "Wait." God has a perfect plan and timing for events in our lives, and we must be patient. That's difficult when the days turn into months that turn into bills that get more and more past due. But we must never doubt God. He will respond when the time is right. (We'll talk more about patience in chapter 7.)

The key is to pray for God's will. "This is the confidence we have in approaching God: that if we ask anything according to his will, he hears us. And if we know that he hears us—whatever we ask—we know that we have what we asked of him" (1 John 5:14-15). While prayer is communication with God, it is important to remember that we are asking according to *God's* will, not *our* will. In reality, we want him to do what is best for us—and what we want at this moment may not be best for us in the long run.

God's ultimate goal for us is to make us more like his Son: "For from the very beginning God decided that those who came to him—and all along he knew who would—*should become like his Son,* so that his Son would be the First, with many brothers" (Romans 8:29, TLB, italics mine). God wants us to be holy as he is holy. He wants us to have an intimate relationship with him; his Spirit within guides us through each step of daily life—and daily life involves major and minor decisions. While God gives us brains that we ought to use, he is never upset by our requests for guidance or help.

PRAYING ABOUT MONEY

So how should you pray during your financial crisis? Warren Wiersbe, in his book *Why Us? When Bad Things Happen to*

God's People, describes three approaches people take toward prayer about suffering.[2]

One approach is to pray to *escape* your suffering. This is natural. Who wouldn't want the financial crisis to be solved immediately? Who isn't tempted to ask God for a miracle million? Jesus prayed that the cup of suffering might be taken away (but it wasn't); Paul prayed that God would take away the physical infirmity that plagued him (but God didn't). The potential problem of praying to escape your financial difficulties is that escape and the quick fix may become the focus, and you're unwilling to listen to God's answers. The hoped-for escape becomes a litmus test as to whether God cares about you and your situation. In all your prayers, God's sovereignty must be humbly recognized and accepted. God may provide an escape one time, yet another time he may not. Either way, he may have some valuable lessons to teach you. Remember, his goal is not to give you a trouble-free life; his goal is to make you more like his Son.

A second approach to prayer during crisis is to pray to *endure* your suffering. While this approach sounds a little more foolproof, it also has its problems. A prayer for endurance focuses all your energy on enduring; it leaves you in a position of maintaining—and you may miss the lessons God wants to teach or growth he wants you to experience. Another problem is that prayer merely to endure may lead you to become proud of your strength and courage; such pride blocks the way for God to mold your character through this crisis. Or you may be able to put on a front of endurance when you're with people and then fall apart at home, which is a subtle kind of hypocrisy.

But there is a third approach to prayer during a crisis— *enlist* your suffering and make it work for you. Wiersbe writes,

If I pray to *escape* suffering, then I'm saying that suffering is my enemy and I must avoid it. But then I may be frustrating the plan of God. If I pray to *endure* suffering, I'm saying that suffering is my master; I'll find myself in bondage when God has created me to be free. If suffering is not to be either my enemy or my master, what is my relationship to suffering? The answer God gave to Paul is *suffering must become your servant.*[3]

How can you make your financial crisis work for you? Wiersbe gives four steps:

Accept the suffering as God's gift.
You may be thinking, *Right. Thanks a lot, Lord.* But acceptance is not the same as resignation. Acceptance is active, a choice you make. You don't escape or simply endure; you work through it. Wiersbe says, "All of this, of course, is an act of faith, and it must come from the heart. If we aren't yet willing to accept what God has given us, we must then ask him to 'make us willing to be made willing.' The longer we oppose God, the more opportunities we lose for receiving his blessings and ministering to others."[4]

Can you accept your financial crisis as part of God's plan for your life? Can you turn to him and say, "Let's work through this together, God"? Can you face the challenge God has given by allowing him to strengthen your faith?

Surrender what God has given by giving it back to him.
God doesn't give you a heavy burden only to watch you stumble beneath it. Jesus promised to help carry your burdens. Can you give your financial crisis and the pain you feel back to God? Can you surrender to him your plans, your pain, your worry, your anger, your fear, your guilt? Can you let go so he can work?

Listen for God's message.
Paul prayed three times that God would take away his thorn in the flesh. God was silent for a while, but then the answer came. God said no, but that his grace was sufficient for Paul and that his power would be made perfect through Paul's weakness (2 Corinthians 12:7-10).

Can you trust that God will answer you? Can you accept his answer and listen for the lessons he wants you to learn?

Live for God's glory.
In the midst of your crisis, God is working. If you're going to grow closer to God and learn more about him, you have to keep on moving and living. You can't hide in your house, pull down the shades, and wait for a miracle. Instead, you need to live as God wants you to live, even as you work through your crisis.

Can you keep on trusting God enough to live for him in the middle of your crisis? In the middle of your crisis, can you glorify God?

Is it OK to pray about money? Yes. In the middle of your financial crisis, as in any crisis or suffering, God wants you to run to him. You need help; ask for it. You need guidance; pray for wisdom. You need an attitude check; ask God to do it. You need a shoulder to cry on; God has a big shoulder. You need someone to talk it all over with; God is an excellent counselor who comes free of charge. If you caused the financial problem you're in, ask God to forgive you and to help you learn his lessons well so it won't happen again.

I previously quoted the first part of Hebrews 4:16. The entire verse reads, "Let us therefore come boldly to the throne of grace, *that we may obtain mercy and find grace to help in time of need*" (NKJV, italics mine).

When you come to God's throne in prayer, you won't receive

a terse "You got yourself into this; get yourself out!" Instead, you are promised mercy, God's loving-kindness that comforts and forgives in spite of stupidity and sinfulness. At God's throne you will find grace, God's undeserved favor, that will help in your time of need.

These comforting words do not mean that God promises to get you out of the crisis the moment you pray. They do not mean that God will erase the natural consequences of any sin that was committed. Nor do they mean that God will explain why the crisis came. But they do mean one important thing: God cares.

WHEN THERE SEEMS TO BE NO ANSWER

Silence from God is frustrating. What do you do when your prayers seem to bounce off the ceiling?

Seeming silence could simply mean that God's answer is "Wait." There may be lessons he wants you to learn through your crisis or an answer of some sort he wants you to wait for. I've often said, tongue in cheek, that God is a procrastinator. Often it seems that God's answers come at the very last minute. But God doesn't procrastinate—he answers at what he knows to be just the right time. He wants us to wait in patience and faith, trusting that he will provide.

But silence can also indicate that something is wrong in your relationship with God. When Jesus talked to his disciples before his death, he promised, "If you remain in me and my words remain in you, ask whatever you wish, and it will be given you" (John 15:7). We often hear the last part and ignore the conditions. If we want answers to our prayers, we must *remain* in Christ and his words must *remain* in us. Our prayers lose their power if we are not obeying Christ. (Admittedly this is a heavy topic to deal with, especially with your limited energy reserves during your crisis. Nevertheless, the points are well worth your consideration, so mark these pages to reread later if the information is too much to take in at this point.)

What kinds of barriers can block your prayers?

Unconfessed and unrepented sin can be a barrier.
"Surely the arm of the Lord is not too short to save, nor his ear too dull to hear. But your iniquities have separated you from your God; your sins have hidden his face from you, so that he will not hear" (Isaiah 59:1-2).

Are you refusing to confess or repent of a particular sin? While sinlessness is an impossibility because of the sinful human nature, you should not be harboring sins—knowing they are wrong but stubbornly refusing to let go of them. This will separate you from God and be a barrier to your prayers. Talk to God about this. Ask him to reveal any sin to you.

One area to consider, of course (though not the only one), is your finances. If you got into this crisis because of over-spending—no discipline, no thought, no budget—then you definitely need to deal with the root of the problem. Are you trying to "keep up with the Joneses"? Are you spending to impress others? Is it a result of a materialistic attitude or coveting? If you got yourself into serious debt because of a sinful attitude toward possessions and money, you need to repent and be forgiven. Then you should get Christian counsel regarding budgeting (you can start with the plan we'll discuss in the next chapter), and perhaps someone to be accountable to for your revised spending habits.

Disobedience can be a barrier.
"For the eyes of the Lord are on the righteous, and his ears are open to their prayer. But the face of the Lord is against those who do evil" (1 Peter 3:12, NRSV).

34

Are you blatantly disobeying God in any area of your life? Do you know something he wants you to do (or not do), but you're refusing to listen? Such disobedience can be a barrier to your prayers—if you have refused to listen to God's guidance before, why should he give you further guidance?

Wrong motives can be a barrier.
"When you ask, you do not receive, because you ask with wrong motives, that you may spend what you get on your pleasures" (James 4:3).

Why are you praying your particular prayer? What is your true motive? You might as well search yourself thoroughly and honestly because God already knows your heart. You may need to straighten out your motives before God will give you further help.

An uncaring attitude toward others can be a barrier.
"If you close your ear to the cry of the poor, you will cry out and not be heard" (Proverbs 21:13, NRSV).

How easy it is to go crying to God when we face a need, yet ignore the needs of others in our times of plenty. If you have refused to help others, God may refuse to help you.

An unforgiving attitude toward others can be a barrier.
"Whenever you stand praying, forgive, if you have anything against anyone; so that your Father in heaven may also forgive you your trespasses" (Mark 11:25, NRSV).

Are you harboring a grudge? Are you refusing to forgive another's sin against you? Read Jesus' parable in Matthew 18:21-35. You must forgive because God has forgiven you.

That doesn't necessarily mean you have to cancel the debts of everyone who owes you money. Depending on your personal convictions and God's guidance, it may well be appropriate to seek legal help (or in the case of another believer, help from the church) in collecting money rightfully owed to you. Being a forgiving Christian doesn't mean being a doormat; that kind of thinking can put you in a position where you're unable to provide for your family or pay your own debts. God's focus is on your attitude.

Doubt can be a barrier.

"If any of you is lacking in wisdom, ask God, who gives to all generously and ungrudgingly, and it will be given you. But ask in faith, never doubting, for the one who doubts is like a wave of the sea, driven and tossed by the wind; for the doubter, being double-minded and unstable in every way, must not expect to receive anything from the Lord" (James 1:5-8, NRSV).

Do you doubt God's care or concern? Do you doubt that he can or will help you? The opposite of doubt is faith. Remember that your faith is based on who God is and what he promises, not on explanations. If you trust God, it is because you know he can be trusted, even though you may not always understand what he is doing. Pray, trusting and believing that God will answer and that his answer will be in your very best interest and for his ultimate glory.

There's another aspect to this that you may not have considered. *How do you know God isn't answering?* While it is valuable to look inward and make sure that you're on the right track with God, a seeming lack of an answer does not mean that you must be harboring some secret sin even though you can't figure out what it is. Instead, what you think is silence may instead be God's quiet miracles.

Remember Elijah on the mountain? He had just witnessed a miraculous display of God's power on Mount Carmel, then wicked Queen Jezebel threatened to have him killed, and he took off running to Mount Horeb. He hid in a cave, fearing for his life. God came to him, telling him to stand on the mountain, "for the Lord is about to pass by" (1 Kings 19:11). A great wind blew, but that wasn't the Lord's presence. Then came an earthquake, then a fire, but God wasn't in them either. Instead, the Lord came to Elijah in a "gentle whisper" (19:12).

God is with you. He is answering, but you may have to be quiet long enough to hear him.

Who can say what miracles God is performing that you don't know about? Who can say what protection he is giving you that goes unseen? Who knows what new crises *haven't* happened because of his intervention on your behalf?

You want a check in the mail; God is mysteriously multiplying your tomato plants. Your car is still running. Your roof doesn't leak. Your kids' shoes will last another month. That one item you need just went on sale. Your penny jar yielded enough for some groceries. (Don't laugh—I took our penny jar to the bank during one desperate stretch, and the jar yielded sixty dollars! I couldn't believe it!) You might find two dollars' worth of change in your couch or in the car so you can buy milk. Praise the Lord!

Remember the Israelites? Even though God condemned them to wander in the wilderness because of their sinful rebellion against him, he still cared for the little details of their lives. Moses reminded them, "During the forty years that I led you through the desert, your clothes did not wear out, nor did the sandals on your feet" (Deuteronomy 29:5).

Or perhaps you've been praying, but your request has focused only on one kind of answer. God knows better what you need. He may be answering, and you're missing it because he's not giving you the answer you expected.

Get the point? God *is* working! He *is* answering your prayers, but in ways you may not see. If you look around, you may realize some amazing miracles you can thank God for. Other miracles may never be revealed, yet God is providing for you.

KNOWING GOD CARES

You are in a time of need. No matter what its cause or how devastating its results, God wants to help. See for yourself. Read the following verses, then in the space below each verse, write out how it applies to your financial crisis and/or how the verse comforts you.

Is anything too hard for the Lord? (Genesis 18:14)

Good and upright is the Lord; therefore he instructs sinners in his ways. He guides the humble in what is right and teaches them his way. (Psalm 25:8-9)

Your love, O Lord, reaches to the heavens, your faithfulness to the skies. Your righteousness is like the mighty mountains, your justice like the great deep. O Lord, you preserve both man and beast. How priceless is your unfailing love! Both high and low among men find refuge in the shadow of your wings. They feast on the abundance of your house; you give them drink from your river of delights. For with you is the fountain of life; in your light we see light. (Psalm 36:5-9)

Then you will call upon me and come and pray to me, and I will listen to you. You will seek me and find me when you seek me with all your heart. (Jeremiah 29:12-13)

Ask, and it will be given you; search, and you will find; knock, and the door will be opened for you. For everyone who asks receives, and everyone who searches finds, and for everyone who knocks, the door will be opened. Is there anyone among you who, if your child asks for bread, will give a stone? Or if the child asks for a fish, will give a snake? If you then, who are evil, know how to give good gifts to your children, how much more will your Father in heaven give good things to those who ask him! (Matthew 7:7-11, NRSV)

Don't worry about anything; instead, pray about everything; tell God your needs, and don't forget to thank him for his answers. If you do this, you will experience God's peace, which is far more wonderful than the human mind can understand. His peace will keep your thoughts and your hearts quiet and at rest as you trust in Christ Jesus. (Philippians 4:6-7, TLB)

You do not have, because you do not ask God. (James 4:2)

Let him have all your worries and cares, for he is always thinking about you and watching everything that concerns you. (1 Peter 5:7, TLB)

Is it OK to pray about your financial crisis? Absolutely. If you've been wandering from God, allow the crisis to draw you back to him (perhaps that's why it happened). If you've been strong and faithful all along, allow God to mold the parts of your life that he still wants to perfect. Take all the energy that has been going into worrying, fretting, being angry at the perpetrator, or feeling guilty, and throw it all into prayer. By all means, yell for help and grab the life jacket!

Talk to God about every aspect of your situation and your feelings about each one. Pray specifically, pray constantly, pray knowing that God will answer.

CHAPTER 4

PLAN

*Failing to plan is the same
as planning to fail*

Planning ahead + having discipline
+ considering the cost = living within your means
LARRY BURKETT

You've gotten a perspective on your financial situation and learned to handle it without falling apart. You've begun faithfully working it through with God. But the bills still arrive in the mail, and you know they must be handled. Your next step is to develop a plan for getting out of debt.

In chapter 5 we'll look at different ways of trimming the fat in your budget and/or adding some extra income. Before we do that, however, we need to sit down, open all those bills, and figure out the numbers. As painful as it may be, this is vital if you're going to come up with a system that can work for you. The bills won't pay themselves; you have to do it, and you have to figure out how it's going to happen.

For some people, a few cutbacks will be enough to pull them out of a crisis; the dollars saved may catch them up on their bills and balance their budget *if* they can make a bill-paying plan and follow it. For others, while the dollars saved are important, they represent only a drop in the bucket against the big, looming bills. Sam still has those credit-card bills to pay—those won't go away, and they keep racking up interest. Lloyd and Karen still have the past-due accounts to clear up. Mitch and Carol face huge medical expenses. There's no way around it. The bills have to be paid. The best way to do it is to develop a plan.

DEVELOPING A PLAN TO PAY YOUR BILLS

I highly recommend *The Financial Planning Workbook,* published by Moody Press and written by Larry Burkett of Christian Financial Concepts. His simplified budget planning is extremely helpful in sorting through your monthly bills, and he gives a good system for working off your debts. I have included his system of listing debts in order of amount and then paying them off in my plan below. My ten-step plan focuses on helping you simply get a handle on your crisis; Burkett's book will go further by helping you reestablish your budget so you won't get into this same kind of crisis again and will let you work back into your budget a savings program, entertainment, clothing, and the little extras. The point is, they will be in your *budget.*

The following is a ten-step plan that will help you set priorities in paying your bills as you work your way through your present financial crisis.

Step 1

Gather together all your bills. Get a pencil, a calculator, and a few sheets of paper. If you don't already have a filing system, get some file folders so you can file each type of bill separately. Prepare a file for your utilities, each type of insurance, taxes, medical bills, car payment, each credit card, then any other bills you owe. If you're in business for yourself, you'll need separate folders for the various suppliers to whom you owe money.

You may not want to look at the bills—this may be the most difficult part. But the only way to get out of the crisis is to deal with it one bill at a time.

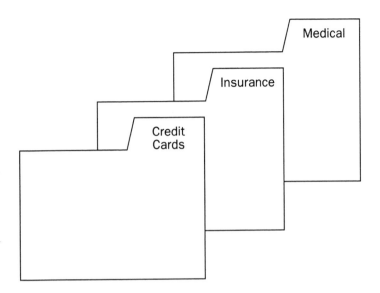

Step 2

On worksheet A (page 50), list your regular monthly bills. On this list, do not include one-time bills that you're working to clear up. Include only those bills that will always be with you or at least are long-term. Your list may look something like this:

Regular Monthly Bills
    Tithes/Pledges
    Mortgage (or Rent)
    Car
    Phone
    Electric
    Gas
    Water
    Car insurance
    Life insurance
    Real estate taxes
    Savings

Step 3

Next, in the space beside each regular monthly bill, list the amount you pay per month. For utilities, write in the average amount per month. For car and life insurance, which are often billed semiannually, figure out how much it would be on a monthly basis and write it in. Then total this list and write that figure on the subtotal line.

This subtotal represents the amount of money you must pay out as your bills arrive every month or should be setting aside in a savings account to be ready when the bill appears (in the case of insurance and sometimes taxes). These are the bills you regularly pay. You have to have money for them, or you will lose something (house, electricity, etc.).

Step 4

The next step is more difficult. Now you need to figure out what needs to be added to the above amount for the following areas:

> Food
> Gas for the car(s)
> Miscellaneous

Write these amounts in the appropriate columns. To figure your food costs, you can use an exercise described in chapter 5 (page 66) to help you find out what you actually spend. You can then work backward to the minimum you think you can get by with. You'll need to fine-tune this, but at least you'll have a figure to work with.

How much gas do you buy? Saving receipts will help keep track of this. If you're not sure right now, fill in your best guess.

The miscellaneous category is different for every family. Maybe it's piano lessons or club dues or your children's allowances. You and your family will have to decide what miscellaneous items are true *needs* and must remain on this list.

If you're in business for yourself or on commission or for some other reason can't count on a particular amount of money every month, you'll need to take a minute and prioritize the categories on worksheet A. For example, the first bills to be paid should always be tithes, the mortgage or rent, and utilities. (In chapter 8, we'll look at questions about tithing when you're in a financial crisis.) Your next priority, especially if you have a family, is to put food on the table. If you're trying to maintain a good credit rating, you'll need to stay on top of loan payments (car, school, personal) and credit-card payments. An argument could be made for cutting back on your savings during an extreme crisis. That will depend on your personal convictions. Pray and discuss it with your family. But setting up a bill-paying priority will make sure your most basic needs are met each month.

Step 5
Now figure out the grand total for the two sets of columns on worksheet A. Here's your vital, bare-bones budget.

Step 6
Now turn to worksheet B (page 51). Use this to list every other bill that you need to clear up (credit cards, medical bills, any other services or places that have extended credit). Lloyd and Karen might have a list like the following:

Clear Up
Hospital
Doctor
Hardware store
Supplier A
Supplier B
Supplier C

Step 7

Go through each bill and write out the total amount that you owe in the "Total Owed" column on worksheet B. This amount will change from month to month as you make payments and as interest charges are added, but for now just write down the amount listed on the most recent bill for each account.

Step 8

After you've put down the totals, rewrite the list in order of the amount owed, starting with the lowest. Generally, this is the order in which you'll pay them off.

In some cases, you may need to list those with higher interest rates, such as credit cards, near the top. You need to try to retire these debts more quickly because of the high interest. (If you have extremely high credit-card debt along with other debt, you may have to consider some other alternatives. See the section "Getting Outside Help" at the end of this chapter.)

In this step, Lloyd and Karen's list may change to:

Supplier B
Hospital
Supplier A
Doctor
Hardware store
Supplier C

Step 9

The only way for Lloyd and Karen—or you—to clear up these bills is to make them manageable. Decide on a standard amount that you can afford to pay on each bill. Credit cards, of course, already have minimum payments that you will want to pay in order to keep up with the interest. You may only be able to afford ten dollars per month on everything else. At least that's a start.

Here's how the "clear up" list works. Let's say that Lloyd and

Karen can put ten dollars toward each bill. They will do that for a couple of months until the first item on the list, "Supplier B," is paid in full. Then the next item, "Hospital," receives the regular ten dollars *plus* the ten dollars that had been going to Supplier B. So the hospital now receives twenty dollars a month. When the hospital is paid, then Supplier A will receive thirty dollars a month, and so on. Without ever changing the budget, every creditor is being paid *something* every month, the smaller bills get paid off more quickly, and, eventually, larger amounts of money become available to pay off the larger bills.

Don't laugh at ten dollars a month. That ten dollars can mean the difference between being left in peace or getting calls from a collection agency threatening you with legal action. If you're making even a small payment every month, at least it shows effort on your part. The creditor knows you're trying. My parents used to own and run a Christian bookstore in a small town. They extended credit to people—some because they were good customers, others because they simply could not buy a Bible otherwise. Some of those poorer customers came in and literally paid one or two dollars a month. Yet that showed my parents that they weren't forgotten. The person wasn't waiting for months to come up with all the money. He or she simply made regular payments. A medical-doctor friend told us he appreciated regular payments, too, no matter how small. Payments of even five dollars a month showed good faith, and that was really what mattered.

The point is, pay *something* every month. Here's how to figure out that amount:

After looking at your bare-bones budget from worksheet A, how much money is left from your paycheck? Work out payments to each of these clear-up bills from that leftover amount. If you don't receive regular paychecks, begin with a minimum amount you think you can afford to pay toward each bill.

Don't let this discourage you. After you've done your bare-bones budget, you may discover that there just isn't any money left. After all, that's why you're in a crisis: There isn't enough money to go around. Maybe some type of supplemental income will be needed. (We'll discuss some possibilities in chapter 5.)

But for now, if there's any money at all available, write how much you can pay toward each bill in the "Amount per Month" column.

Step 10

Finally, turn to worksheet C (page 52). Divide your list of monthly bills according to whether you're paid weekly or bi-weekly, and decide which ones you'll pay out of each paycheck during the month. Check the due dates on each bill and decide, for example, which ones you'll pay with the paycheck from the fifteenth of the month and which you'll pay with the paycheck from the thirty-first. Then fit in your clear-up bills around those other bills. Lloyd and Karen go by the week because they're in business for themselves. Their list looks like this:

	Regular	*Clear Up*
Week One	Tithes Mortgage Health Ins.	
Week Two	Gas Electric Business Ins.	Doctor Hospital Visa
Week Three	Telephone Car Car Insurance	Hardware store Supplier A
Week Four	Water/Sewer Taxes	Supplier B Supplier C

In order to pay for food and gas through the month, it can be a good idea to take out in cash the amount of money budgeted for those items. My parents used to put the cash in labeled envelopes hidden in a safe place. They then drew from these envelopes as needed. Once the money is gone, you can't spend any more until the next paycheck arrives. This keeps you from incurring any new debt.

After you've completed worksheet C, make several photocopies. Use a copy of it as a checklist every month. When you get your paycheck, you'll know exactly which bills to pay. Cross each bill off your list as you pay it. Then, even if you've only paid ten dollars toward a certain bill, you paid your quota for the month, you've crossed it off, and it's done with. *Don't worry about it anymore.* You "paid" it.

Write the amount you paid on your portion of each bill and file it in the appropriate file. Then you can keep track of your payments. Check to see that you received credit for that payment on your next bill.

After you've worked out a budget, you need to notify the creditors about how much you plan to pay each month. This can be as simple as writing it on the bill when you send back a payment. Apologize for your tardiness, express your willingness to pay the bill, and explain that you will be sending x number of dollars each month until more money is freed up in order to retire the debt more quickly. Then *keep to that payment schedule.*

From this moment, work from your bare-bones budget. Then as new ideas surface or money comes in from selling items or from another job, the money can be used to retire the lower debt(s), and you can then put larger amounts into the larger debts.

WORKSHEET A

My Regular Monthly Bills	Amount per Month
_____	_____
_____	_____
_____	_____
_____	_____
_____	_____
_____	_____
_____	_____
_____	_____
_____	_____
_____	_____
_____	_____
_____	_____
_____	_____
_____	_____
Subtotal	_____

OTHER EXPENSES — Amount per Month

	Amount per Month
Food	_____
Gas for the car(s)	_____
Miscellaneous	_____
Subtotal	_____
GRAND TOTAL	_____

WORKSHEET B

Bills I'm Going to Clear Up   **Total Owed**

_____   _____
_____   _____
_____   _____
_____   _____
_____   _____
_____   _____
_____   _____
_____   _____
_____   _____
_____   _____
_____   _____
_____   _____

Rewrite the above list in order of amount owed (lowest to highest):

Name   **Total Owed**   **Amount per Month**

_____   _____   _____
_____   _____   _____
_____   _____   _____
_____   _____   _____
_____   _____   _____
_____   _____   _____
_____   _____   _____
_____   _____   _____
_____   _____   _____
_____   _____   _____
_____   _____   _____
_____   _____   _____

WORKSHEET C

Monthly Bill Payment Schedule

	Regular	Clear Up
Paycheck #1		
Paycheck #2		

OR

	Regular	Clear Up
Week One		
Week Two		
Week Three		
Week Four		

PLAYING WITH PLASTIC

Perhaps the most important step during this process is to decide with your family that you will accumulate no new debt. But what about all those magical plastic cards in your wallet? They make so many promises; they make every desire so easy to obtain. But how dangerous are they to your budget?

Howard L. Dayton, founder of Crown Ministries, in an article called "How to Get Out of Debt," writes:

> The only way I know to accumulate no new debt is to pay for everything with cash or check at the time of purchase. This raises the issue of credit cards. I do not believe credit cards are sinful, but they are dangerous. Americans carry over 700 million of them, and only 30 percent of their charge accounts are paid in full each month. It has been statistically shown that people spend approximately one-third more when they use credit cards rather than cash. Here's the rule of thumb: If you always pay the entire monthly balance due, you can probably handle your credit cards. If you do not, they are too dangerous for you. In that case, I suggest you perform plastic surgery—any good pair of scissors will do.[1]

Dayton says it best. The only way to keep from using your cards is to get rid of them. Most financial counselors require their clients to cut up the cards before any counseling even begins. There's no point in trying to get out of debt on one end while adding it up on the other. There's nothing more stupid (from a financial standpoint) than to use credit cards for cash advances (at interest rates above 19 percent) in order to pay off debts with lower interest or no interest (such as medical bills), or for purchases that have no long-term value (groceries, movies, dinners out, etc.).

Checking of the numbers can bring you into harsh reality. The average credit-card holder is carrying a $2000 balance at 18 percent interest and is making minimum payments. At that rate of payment, it will take more than twelve years to pay off the balance, even if the card goes unused during that time! And here's the kicker—total *interest* paid would come to $2,231.[2]

You *can* get by without credit cards. In your financial situation, you must at least stop using them until you're out of debt. Cancel the cards that carry an annual fee and you're already saving $20–$35 a year. (Cut up the card and mail it back to the company to make sure the charge doesn't get automatically added to an upcoming bill.)

If you feel you need some kind of major credit card, consider a debit card (available from both Visa and MasterCard). You can get one through your bank or credit union. These plastic cards look like credit cards, but they work like cash or a check so there's no way to run up a debt. Before you can make a purchase with your debit card, the money has to be in the bank. This avoids impulse purchases, interest fees, and the deadly bill arriving at the end of the month.

There are two kinds of debit cards. An "on-line" debit card is like an ATM card. At the point of purchase, a computer automatically checks to see if you have enough money in the bank to cover the purchase. If so, the money is withdrawn from the account that same day. If not, the purchase is refused. An "off-line" debit card works like a check. The store sends a record of the transaction to your bank, and the money is withdrawn from the account a few days later. Both cards can be used wherever Visa or MasterCard is accepted.

Most banks offer debit cards free of charge, although some might impose an annual fee, a fee for each transaction, or require a minimum balance in the account. You may receive a checkbook as well, so checks can also be written on the account. Be careful to remember to record any purchases made with the debit card so you always know your balance.

It's a great feeling when you get through Christmas debt free! Stand in line when you do your Christmas shopping and watch everyone around you add up debt while you, on the other hand, pay cash—knowing that in January there will be no new debts on your credit-card bills.

It isn't easy to do that. Especially if the credit cards are available to you. Everyone wants to buy nice gifts at Christmas, and the credit card makes virtually anything available to you. If there isn't enough cash, just put it on the card! But you'll be hurting when the bill arrives.

One particularly rough Christmas, we had only five dollars to spend on each of our three kids. My husband did the shopping and came home with two toys for each child (I still don't know how he did it). We made a tree out of lots of sheets of green construction paper stuck on the wall (Buy a tree? Forget it!) and added "ornaments" (round circles of other colors of paper). The kids decorated; I tried to be cheerful. That year, the gifts from relatives and those little gifts from Sunday school teachers were especially appreciated! It was very humbling; I had to focus on the spirit of Christmas and not the material part. I could go without gifts myself, but I hated to see my kids go without. I had to pray a lot that year about my attitude and about talking to my children about the most important gift of all.

GETTING OUTSIDE HELP

Is all this paperwork and figuring over your head? Does it sound like a good idea but you don't think you can do it? Would you have a hard time working this out with your spouse? What if there simply is no way to bring in extra cash—or no amount of extra cash that can make a dent in your debt? Don't despair. Help is available. You just need to have the courage to ask.

Maybe it's as simple as getting a trusted family member or friend to help you work through the system explained above. Maybe a short-term, low-interest loan from a family member could pay off the most burdensome debts or serve to consolidate your debts into one payment back to that person. But most people don't want to divulge the secrets of their bank accounts to *anyone* they know. In some cases, it's wisest *not* to be a borrower or a lender (to loosely quote Shakespeare).

An accountant may be able to help you (just be sure you can afford his or her services). Your bank may offer some kind of credit counseling or debt-consolidation service. There are also companies that can help. However, before you go with any credit counselor, confirm that the agency is truly nonprofit. There are plenty of companies that want to consolidate your debts and handle your finances, but you may find yourself involved with a rip-off artist or with a company that will charge hundreds of dollars in fees and not be able to do anything because your creditors won't deal with that company.

The National Foundation for Consumer Credit is a nonprofit umbrella organization that monitors more than eight hundred local offices nationwide (Consumer Credit Counseling Service offices) that handle budget and credit counseling. (To find their agencies in your city, check the white pages in your phone book under "Consumer Credit Counseling Services," or call the national referral line at 1-800-388-2227.) Offices affiliated with NFCC can often negotiate with your creditors for you, lowering an interest payment or stretching out a term to work out a payment plan that you can manage. You then will pay a monthly lump sum into a trust fund from which the agency will parcel out agreed-upon payments to creditors. All of this is done for a nominal fee.

If your credit-card debt is so high that you can barely meet the minimum payments, you'll have to pay these off first; they need to be at the top of your list on worksheet B. The problem is that if the credit cards are at the top of your list, but you only make minimum payments, you'll never get anywhere. The minimum payments on your bills barely cover the interest each month, so you never actually work down the debt. That means you can never pay it off in order to work on your other debts. Decide right now that you'll focus your energies on getting rid of those credit-card bills. Whatever extra money comes in—whatever you sell, your income tax refund—should be applied right away to the credit cards to bring down the balance, bring down the interest, and eventually pay off the bill.

Primerica Financial Services suggests taking out a debt-consolidation loan by using the equity in your home to pay off all debts (especially credit-card debt). Yes, you do have a loan to pay back, but it is at a much lower interest rate, you can pay back one lump sum every month, you know how much the payments will be, you know how to budget the payments, you know when you'll be out of debt, and you even get a tax deduction. However, don't even think about taking out such a loan if you're not committed to staying out of debt. This would definitely mean cutting up the credit cards and living on cash only.

What about declaring bankruptcy? Like our country's welfare system, bankruptcy can be a safety net to keep people from getting so far down financially that they can never recover. But, also like welfare, bankruptcy is abused by many who needn't or shouldn't use it. You should consider this only as a last resort; it is *not* a quick cure-all for your financial problems.

There are far more advantages to paying off your debts (no matter how slowly) than filing for bankruptcy and facing its consequences. To begin bankruptcy proceedings, you'll need a lawyer, who will charge you an up-front fee (usually well over five hundred dollars). You can then give the lawyer's name and number to any creditors that call, and the lawyer will handle all calls for you—and the harassing calls will stop one by one. A court takes over the administration of your finances, and court dates are set to check on your personal assets. Bankruptcy can entail surrendering all your assets, including your home, cars, and personal property, although most state laws allow people to keep a certain amount. Creditors are invited to bankruptcy proceedings, all of which are public. A bankruptcy will remain on your credit report for up to ten years, making it impossible to buy a house or a car, finance your child's education, or get any kind of credit anywhere. It can also reflect poorly on you when you try to get a job or obtain an apartment.

Remember that as a Christian you are ethically obligated to repay what you rightfully owe to creditors. Buying on credit includes a promise to repay. The writer of Proverbs saw the situation clearly: "The borrower is servant to the lender" (Proverbs 22:7). Bankruptcy should never be used as an easy out so that you can start the process over again and ring up more debt. Too often people reach for the quick fix—just erasing debts—rather than facing a couple of years of belt-tightening in order to pay what they owe to others. It may take a long time and lots of sacrifice in order to pay those debts, but it is the right thing to do. As a Christian, consider that God would have you pay your debts without reaching for the quick fix. Steer clear of bankruptcy if at all possible.

Obviously, Christians should never run up debt, intending to file bankruptcy to get out of paying. The psalmist wrote: "The wicked borrow and do not repay" (Psalm 37:21). Our true character often shows most clearly in how we handle our money. Don't file for bankruptcy just to get away from the stress your bills cause you.

But in some situations, bankruptcy—even with all its consequences—may be the only way to protect yourself from losing your home and being unable to provide for your family. If you consider bankruptcy, you must honestly weigh your motivations and your goals. You must carefully consider your personal situation. Get good legal counsel, and make sure you understand all the consequences.

After you've taken a good hard look at the numbers, you'll need to work on setting or changing some financial priorities. Let's consider these in the next chapter.

CHAPTER 5
PRIORITIES
Wealth is relative—now what I need is a rich relative!

A good mind possesses a kingdom;
a great fortune is a great slavery.
SENECA

I have never liked the book of Job—in fact, I avoid it as much as possible. I think I don't like to face up to the book's main point: People suffer and God may never explain why. Like a child I stamp my foot and say, "That's not fair, God!" Why should Job have to suffer so much just so God could make a point? It sure seems that God didn't care. And even when the end of suffering came and Job asked for an explanation, all he got was a lecture.

But I err right at the start in even thinking to compare myself to Job. I doubt that God would hold me up as a shining example of righteousness as he did Job. Indeed, he said of Job, "There is no one on earth like him; he is blameless and upright, a man who fears God and shuns evil" (Job 1:8). Job had great wealth: "He owned seven thousand sheep, three thousand camels, five hundred yoke of oxen and five hundred donkeys, and had a large number of servants. He was the greatest man among all the people of the East" (Job 1:3). Job had great wealth, but he also loved, worshiped, and obeyed the one true God.

Job had his priorities right.

SETTING PRIORITIES ABOUT MONEY

You might be saying, "Right! This guy had more riches than he knew what to do with. Sure, I'd have no problem being a great Christian if I didn't have to worry so much about money and paying the bills!"

Well, Satan had the same idea. He figured that Job worshiped God because God had blessed him so much. Satan said, "Let me take all that stuff away, make him poor, and he'll sing another tune."

So God let Satan launch his attack. Enemy tribes stole all the livestock and killed all the servants; a storm knocked down the house where all Job's sons and daughters were feasting, killing them all.

Think for a minute. Job lost *all his wealth* in one day. He then also lost *all his children*. Does that put your crisis in perspective? If anyone can be an example to us by living through his own crisis, Job can. What did Job do? "In all this, Job did not sin by charging God with wrongdoing" (Job 1:22).

Job didn't say, "But God, I thought we had a deal here. I act righteously, and you heap blessings on me." Instead, Job said, "The Lord gave, and the Lord has taken away; Blessed be the name of the Lord" (Job 1:21, NKJV).

Job understood something we often forget. God doesn't promise goodies when we become believers. He offers great blessings, many received in this life, most in the next. He never promised that every believer will have (and never lose) his own home, that every believer would always have enough money to pay all the bills, that every believer would never lose a job and face difficult times, that every believer would receive his or her version of justice in this life.

The health-and-wealth gospel has received lots of press—who doesn't want to hear that God wants you to be rich? The only problem is, it is dead wrong. God does not promise riches—in fact, the Bible constantly tells about the inherent dangers of great wealth, for it tends to make people feel self-sufficient and independent of God. Listen to what Scripture says about the dangers of wealth:

> Be careful. . . . Otherwise, when you eat and are satisfied, when you build fine houses and settle down, and when your herds and flocks grow large and your silver and gold increase and all you have is multiplied, then your heart will become proud and you will forget the Lord your God. (Deuteronomy 8:11-14)

> Wealth is worthless in the day of wrath. . . . Whoever trusts in his riches will fall. (Proverbs 11:4, 28)

> Whoever loves money never has money enough; whoever loves wealth is never satisfied with his income. (Ecclesiastes 5:10)

> They will throw their silver into the streets, and their gold will be an unclean thing. Their silver and gold will not be able to save them in the day of the Lord's wrath. They will not satisfy their hunger or fill their stomachs with it, for it has made them stumble into sin. (Ezekiel 7:19)

> No one can serve two masters. . . . You cannot serve both God and Money. (Matthew 6:24)

> For what will it profit them if they gain the whole world but forfeit their life? Or what will they give in return for their life? (Matthew 16:26, NRSV)

> But woe to you who are rich, for you have already received your comfort. (Luke 6:24)

And [Jesus] said to them, "Take care! Be on your guard against all kinds of greed; for one's life does not consist in the abundance of possessions." (Luke 12:15, NRSV)

But God said to him, "You fool! This very night your life will be demanded from you. Then who will get what you have prepared for yourself?" This is how it will be with anyone who stores up things for himself but is not rich toward God. (Luke 12:20-21)

Jesus looked at him and said, "How hard it is for the rich to enter the kingdom of God!" (Luke 18:24)

For of this you can be sure: No . . . greedy person . . . has any inheritance in the kingdom of Christ and of God. (Ephesians 5:5)

For the love of money is a root of all kinds of evil. Some people, eager for money, have wandered from the faith and pierced themselves with many griefs. . . . Command those who are rich in this present world not to be arrogant nor to put their hope in wealth, which is so uncertain, but to put their hope in God. . . . Command them to do good, to be rich in good deeds, and to be generous and willing to share. (1 Timothy 6:10, 17-18)

The brother in humble circumstances ought to take pride in his high position. But the one who is rich should take pride in his low position, because he will pass away like a wild flower. (James 1:9-10)

Now listen, you rich people, weep and wail because of the misery that is coming upon you. Your wealth has rotted, and moths have eaten your clothes. Your gold and silver are corroded. Their corrosion will testify against you and eat your flesh like fire. You have hoarded wealth in the last days. . . . You have lived on earth in luxury and self-indulgence. You have fattened yourselves in the day of slaughter. (James 5:1-3, 5)

Get the picture? God had lots to say about wealth, and usually it wasn't flattering. Why? Not because money in itself is bad, but because God knows the power of money and how easily it entices us into all kinds of sin.

You may be saying, "But I'm not asking to be rich—I just want enough to meet my needs." That's really the issue: What are *truly* your *needs?*

SETTING PRIORITIES IN DAILY LIFE

If we really wanted to get to basics, the only needs every human being has are air, food, water, and shelter. But our complex world rarely allows us to deal in basics only, so let's expand that by considering a balanced life. As human beings we have

- physical needs: a healthy diet, a certain amount of cleanliness, shelter, and clothing suitable to our environment
- social and emotional needs: friendships, family relationships, manners
- spiritual needs: a personal relationship with God
- intellectual needs: such as the ability to read, understand language, and communicate

Chances are that your financial crisis is putting a crunch on the area of meeting physical needs. You can meet social, spiritual, and intellectual needs for free. You can get together with friends over popcorn. You can continue to fellowship at your church and have your devotions and daily relationship with God. You can go to the library to read current newspapers and magazines. But unless you live off the land in a handmade cabin with only a ham radio connecting you to the outside world, you probably have lots of expenses in the "physical needs" category. Let's consider some areas where we need to set priorities in order to meet these needs.

First, let's look at the difference between needs and desires.

Food

We all need food. We could have a healthy diet with rice and bread, vegetables, fruit, milk, small amounts of meat, and water. Not necessarily an expensive diet. But it's difficult to set priorities and pare down a larder that is usually full of cookies, convenience foods, soda pop, and every other frill offered by the giants in food manufacturing. Yet you need to take a hard look at how much money you spend on food. Figure in

- your major trips to the grocery store
- every side trip (the ones where you go to get "one thing" and come home with five)
- eating out (such as school and office lunches and snacks)

As an interesting exercise, keep track of every expense on food, down to the penny, for a week or two. You'll be surprised at how much you spend—even on your tight budget. Then study your register receipts (if they describe the items purchased; otherwise study your grocery list, as long as you add all the items you bought that *weren't* originally on the list). From there, you can see more clearly where you can trim.

My purpose here is not to give you "101 Ways to Trim Your Food Budget." Such creative and helpful lists abound in women's magazines, and you can find them at the library. (Don't *buy* any—you're on a limited budget, remember?) I simply want to illustrate that it can and must be done—and food is the first place to start because it's a huge chunk of most families' budgets. But what you think you need may only be what you desire (or crave or want or are used to buying). I highly recommend Amy Dacyczyn's book, *The Tightwad Gazette: Promoting Thrift As a Viable Alternative* (Villard Books, 1993). It is full of ways to cut costs in your daily living. You'll be amazed at how many ways you can be more frugal and maybe even have fun while you're doing it! Another book you might check into is Mike Yorkey's *Saving Money Any Way You Can* (Servant Publications, 1994).

Cleanliness
My mom always said, "No matter how poor you are, you can always be clean!" I think the statement is not only true, but very wise. You may be going through a difficult financial crisis, but people don't need to smell it on you! In other words, you want to feel good about yourself through the crisis, so don't skimp on taking care of your body (and those of your family members). That's all pretty obvious; however, the rub comes when you need to consider that, for now, you can't afford the shampoo from the salon or a new shade of lipstick. Again, what you think you need may only be what you desire.

Clothing
What about our clothing "needs"? If you have teenagers, you already know about this problem. But once again, what you think you need may only be what you desire. You may have to clean up those old gym shoes and polish the dress shoes. Last year's summer clothes may have to get you through another summer. Your children may need to take advantage of hand-me-

downs or resale-shop clothing. What you really need is far less than what you want. Lots of magazines give inexpensive ideas for sprucing up your wardrobe or breathing new life into old clothes. Take advantage of such tips and ideas. You might even have fun.

Shelter

Human beings have the basic need for shelter, and it comes in all styles and sizes. This may be the hardest bill of all to pay. Obviously it would save money if you lived on the streets, but that's not a viable option. You do have options, though. You'll have to look for them and be creative. Books have been written about handling your major assets during a time of crisis, and you may need to get some expert advice. Perhaps just a few changes can help solve the problem and get you through the crisis. You will have to consider your specific situation from all vantage points, and you will need to discuss with your family what can work best for your situation. Some adjustments are major, some are minor; some are permanent, some are temporary. For instance:

- Can you refinance your mortgage to lower the payments? (This may help, although refinancing can cost money up front and can affect your taxes. Get good advice when considering this option.)
- Could you tap into your home's equity for some needed cash or to obtain a debt-consolidation loan? (Again, get advice when considering this option.)
- Could you rent out a room in your house or apartment?
- Or be more creative—do you have extra space in a garage that you could rent to someone as storage or work space?

These are difficult decisions that must be made carefully,

thoughtfully, often with the advice of experts, and with the consensus of others involved (your family). You may not want a roommate, but for a time, you might need one. You might not want to rent out a room of your home, but would a few months of extra income help?

Next, consider cutting back on some of the other bills that go along with your shelter—such as your utilities. A few degrees on the thermostat translate into dollars saved over the course of time. Consider your water and electricity usage. What can you do to save some here and some there? Again, magazines abound with ideas for pinching pennies in the household. Get some ideas and try them out.

Transportation

Transportation is another basic need in our busy world. And again, there are numerous options for cutting back on what you spend in this area. You and your family will have to decide what will work for you. You may not be able to sell that brand-new second car because of financing, but perhaps you can let it go by having someone else take over the payments (get good advice on how to handle this). If that second car is old, can you sell it for a few extra dollars—and can your family live without it? Can the kids ride bikes or walk? What about carpooling to work?

If you use public transportation, try to be creative and find the least expensive alternative. Can you ride a bicycle to the train station, thus saving gas and parking fees? Will a monthly bus or subway pass be cheaper than paying every day? What parts of your route can you walk instead of ride? You may find that a few extra cents translate into a lot of money when multiplied by five days a week, fifty-two weeks a year!

The extras

What about bills that don't even fit into the basics? Consider that health-club membership and how much you use it, or cable TV, or the cost of renting videotapes as opposed to borrowing from the library or exchanging with friends. Can you cut back on magazine subscriptions? Where else is there "fat" in your budget?

A word of caution here: A few dollars spent on your emotional well-being are a wise investment. Even though my husband and I have had some really rough times, one thing we protect is a "date night" once every couple of weeks. Yes, we have to pay a baby-sitter (unless we can get Grandma to do it), but we have found that an evening alone together over a hamburger helps us to communicate and discuss ideas. Probably some of the best dates are the nights when we don't talk about our troubles, but instead talk about how lucky we are and how much we love each other and the kids, and when we take time to dream about the future when things will be better. We stay in love, we stay sane, and we're on each other's team. We *know* we can make it through together.

Think of the cutbacks and concessions you have to make as though you're on a diet. Some of the changes will be only temporary; some will be adopted for a lifetime. Will you ever be able to buy cookies again? Yes. Will you ever be able to buy a new sweater again? Yes. Will you ever see a first-run movie again? Of course.

Sam, our fired corporate-headquarters guy from chapter 1, will have to begin here. He will need to trim his budget tremendously, if only for a while. He may have to make some changes in his housing, sell one car (or both and get used ones), and ask for a refund on the fur on layaway. And he will most definitely have to cut up his credit cards.

Then after he's gotten his perspective, he needs to sit down and talk it over with his wife and kids. Communication among family members will alleviate a lot of stress. Like Sam, you can help your family realize that you're in this together, enlist ideas from them about how to set priorities that will trim the expenses, and assure them that some of the more drastic measures may be only temporary. Talk about

- what to give up or cut back on
- for what purpose (how much is saved?)
- for how long

Talk about keeping a perspective on the crisis—use the hints from chapter 2—and be a good example of how to do it. Then pray together. As you crunch numbers and talk about cutbacks, don't ever forget that God is in control.

CREATIVE IDEAS FOR MEETING THE CRISIS

After you've worked through the budget plan described in chapter 4, you may have discovered that you need to think about some more drastic life changes in order to pull through this crisis. But once again, think of them as temporary. Perhaps you've realized that the bottom line is that you need more money on a consistent basis in order to put together a budget that can handle paying off your bills.

First, look for money in other areas—money to which you are entitled that you might not be aware of. For example:

- Are you entitled to unemployment benefits? If you're legally entitled, don't delay applying for this compensation.
- Could you borrow against your life-insurance policy? Could you save on insurance by carrying term insurance rather than whole life? Consult your insurance agent.

- Can you tap into your company's retirement plan?
  Check with your company's accounting office.

While having a garage sale or selling a comic book collection or that motorcycle might give you enough money to help out, often the crisis means your family needs another income in the form of a second job. A second job, or a job for your spouse, can take on a variety of colors. Before you explore this option, you need to consider the impact on your health and your family and be willing to think creatively.

If you have young children, you'll want to try to work around each other's schedules so one of you can be home with them and save the cost of a baby-sitter. Can one of you work evenings? Can one of you cut back daytime hours and work at home in order to allow the other an afternoon/evening shift? Many jobs offer evening shifts; some jobs can only be done after hours, such as cleaning offices.

While you may be saying, "But my husband (wife) and I will never see each other!" remember, once again, that you're talking about a *temporary* measure. The second job is only to help with the bills that need to be paid off. *Earmark the money so that you don't raise your standard of living to match the money coming in.* Use the second income *only* to work with the crisis budget you prepared in chapter 4 and to pay off the past-due bills. Then, when you get the bills paid or the budget under control, you're free to stop or cut back on working if you choose.

Besides going out to look for a job, another option is working at home. Do you have a talent or expertise you could "sell"? All kinds of jobs can be done out of your home—perhaps you could edit, proofread, tutor, type, do accounting, or prepare taxes; maybe you could make and sell craft projects, repair cars or small engines, sew and/or mend; or depending on the laws in your state, you could do some form of child care in your home.

Sometimes teenagers can help out. You could have your kids contribute some of the money they earn by mowing lawns, shoveling snow, housecleaning for others, or doing odd jobs. They could contribute to the family budget some of the money they earn at a part-time job or simply use the money they earn for their own expenses—clothes and other basics.

If you're going to get your kids involved, you'll need to tell them the situation, let them know the numbers involved, and make them understand the confidentiality of your family situation. You can help them see what the money they contribute accomplishes in the budget.

This can be an excellent learning experience. All teenagers would do well to learn early the value of money—how hard it is to earn and how quickly it goes. Many just don't know how much is needed for basics like housing and electricity and car insurance. They take it for granted that those things are always there. You might let them help you write out the checks one month so they can see where the money is going and how fast a paycheck dwindles. Perhaps then they'll realize that when Mom and Dad say they just can't afford those hundred-dollar gym shoes, Mom and Dad are really telling the truth. Or that the twenty dollars they contribute each month pays the water bill—and that's a big help for the family because it keeps the water from being shut off.

As you think about various options, take the time to crunch numbers and communicate with one another about all aspects:

How will the family be affected by the change?
Can the new job or new responsibilities be handled so that the home still runs smoothly? Can everyone still be healthy and happy? If one parent has to miss a son's basketball games

temporarily, can the other parent make it? Can the games be videotaped? Granted, there will have to be a few sacrifices if you want to get out of your crisis, but if you are careful with your budget, the sacrifices will only be temporary. You and your family will have to talk about what sacrifices can be handled. Communication is key.

Is a second job worth the added expense it will involve?
Even if a second job pays well, will you need a new wardrobe, baby-sitter, and transportation in order to take the job? How much money would be left after those additional expenses? Is the job then worth it?

Can you discipline yourselves to stay on your budget?
Remember that as you consider ways to meet present needs, you must be careful not to slip into a higher standard of living. Once you get a handle on how much you're earning (if you're self-employed, don't forget about the taxes you'll need to pay on that income), apply that amount to the bills to be paid off. While you're certainly justified in allowing your family a pizza night once in a while, don't get into the trap of using the added income to buy extras.

Can you make the necessary permanent changes?
Remember that while you're on a temporary course of action to get out of debt, the lesson you need to learn must be permanent. You don't want to pay off the bills only to get your credit cards back and start the cycle all over again. That's why most financial counselors will insist that you cut up your credit cards and not obtain any more. Credit-card debt is often the most costly, the easiest to run up, and the most difficult to pay off (as you may already know!). The pain you're experiencing is probably lesson enough, but you and your family must make a commitment not only to *get* out of debt but also to *stay* out of debt.

Once you're out of debt, revise your crisis budget for a regular budget. Check your Christian bookstore for books on budgeting and money management.

What can you put into savings?
Finally, make a commitment to build a savings account—even if you start with only a few dollars a month. Most credit counselors suggest that you have enough money in savings to cover three months of your bare-bones budget. Then, if a crisis occurs, you've got money in the bank to meet your family's basic needs without turning to credit cards again.

KEEPING LIFE IN BALANCE

This chapter is about setting priorities. As you work on setting priorities that will get you out of your present crisis, don't forget about the other priorities in life: social and emotional needs, spiritual needs, and intellectual needs. While your priorities may shift a little, you still must keep your life balanced.

When it all comes down to the basics, you are God's child and God cares about you. The book of Job ends with these words, "The Lord blessed the latter part of Job's life more than the first" (Job 42:12). Why? Because through all his trials, Job affirmed his faith in God. As you struggle through your personal crisis, keep your eyes focused on God, the only one who knows the outcome, the only one who knows the work he wants to do in your life. Rely on God's strength; make him your solid foundation.

Job had his priorities right; so can you.

CHAPTER 6

PRIDE
A head held high can look up to God

An inferiority complex would be a blessing,
if only the right people had it.
ALAN REED

Let's pretend for a minute that you're a world-class swimmer. But if you fall off a ship into the ocean, even you would be unable to hold up against the endless smashing of the huge waves. When the people on the ship toss you a life preserver, you say to yourself, *Hey, I'm a world-class swimmer! I don't need a life preserver; I can make it on my own.*

Pretty silly, right? Your pride could cause you to drown. Yet that's what happens too often with people in financial crisis. The crisis hits, and you feel like you ought to be able to weather it alone. You would rather die than tell anyone you don't have grocery money.

It is important for you to keep a certain amount of pride. I'm talking about good pride—positive self-esteem that shows that you remember your importance to God, that you understand the value of hard work, and that your crisis does not make you a lesser person. While your self-esteem takes a beating as you deal with bill collectors and beg for leniency, you can still *have* self-esteem because you know you're doing your best.

But what if you've already lost whatever self-esteem you had? What if your situation has put you into a downward spiral of depression? What if you're feeling that you are inadequate because you can't provide for your family? Sam could slide downward if he allows himself to fret over the fact that he can no longer provide the comfortable lifestyle to which he and his family are accustomed. Ruth could slip into deep depression over her husband's desertion, feeling that she is somehow at fault.

Losing self-esteem is a serious matter. It makes it difficult for you to get out of bed and face each new day. It allows the crisis to immobilize you so that you can't move beyond it.

It is possible to regain your lost self-esteem—even in the depths of your crisis. Losing a loved one, a job, a paycheck, or possessions happens outside of us; self-esteem happens *inside*. You can regain lost self-esteem if you turn to the only one who knows you inside out: God.

If you have not accepted Christ as your personal Savior, you need to do so, for only then will you find a solid foundation for your life. Ask God to make himself real to you. If you already are a Christian, trust God to work through your circumstances to develop you into the person he wants you to be. Your personal relationship with Christ enables you to withstand life's ebbs and flows. While your self-esteem may have disintegrated, your value to God has never changed. Remember that you are important to God because you are his child. Ask him to remind you daily that you have been chosen by him as his very own. Your value is based on what God has done for you.

God wants you to have positive self-esteem. He doesn't want you depressed or beating on yourself. Talk to God. Read Scripture to remind yourself of his incredible love for you. If you need help, find a Christian counselor, pastor, or friend who can help you. You can get out of bed each day knowing that you have a job to do for God—worshiping, serving, praising, using the gifts he has given, and trusting him to provide. Our ultimate goal in life is to be like Christ. Do not compare yourself to anyone but him. Ask him for guidance. Pray for provision. Trust him to guide you in the way that is best for you to go. Hold your head high—you are a child of the King! Enter the throne room and ask him to help you regain self-esteem so that you can keep on following him in order to move beyond the crisis.

As you seek to meet your responsibilities, you might find yourself needing to call on other sources for help. This will butt up against the negative kind of pride: being unwilling to let others see that you have a need. But the fact is, if you can't feed your family, you need to ask someone to help you do so. God's ideal, as expressed in his Word, is that your extended family come to your aid. In the absence of family, or if your family can't help, the extended family of the church can offer help in a time of need.

So how can you have self-esteem, but not be too proud to ask for help? How can you hold your head high during your crisis?

JUDGE NOT . . .

There are a thousand reasons *not* to ask people for help. You know people will sit in judgment. Mitch and Carol don't dare ask for help; already one lady in the church snapped at them about being irresponsible with their money—playing around instead of getting health insurance. She told them that their problem was God's judgment on them.

Ouch!

Then there's Sam. Despite the fact that he is probably the only church member who gives above and beyond the tithe, does so cheerfully, and has single-handedly helped carry their small church's budget when everyone else was slacking off in giving, the people sort of smirk to see him in a tight position. "Did you hear he might have to sell that Mercedes?" someone asks. "He can't get that fur for his wife, poor thing," says a catty voice. Some are glad to see that he has to experience real life, so to speak.

You've been in on conversations like this. Here are some other forms the gossip (sometimes thinly disguised as "shared concern" in Christian circles) might take:

> "I'm so tired of hearing that family whine about their needs. They *always* seem to have some crisis or another. I don't know how many times we've bailed them out and they just come back with another problem. Sometimes I think they just want a free ride at our expense."

> "Did you hear about so-and-so? He just lost his job, and now they can't keep up those house payments. Well, I always thought that house was too expensive anyway. They got in over their heads, and now I guess they're getting what they deserve."

> "You know, I lent so-and-so money and he hasn't paid it back, but I just saw him in a new pair of expensive running shoes. What's he doing hitting up his friends for money if he can afford things like that?"

> "So-and-so just got a huge raise. I wonder what she does with all that money she makes—besides buying *very* expensive clothes. She sure doesn't give much to the church."

And on and on. . . . Some of the complaints are legitimate, some smack of a bad attitude, and all are based on misunderstanding and misinformation. But what it comes down to is very simple: No one has the right to judge anyone else's financial situation. I say that with the understanding that some people truly do need to be disciplined by the church in that area; some people do need to be confronted by loving friends. But too often, complaints and gossip begin because someone who doesn't understand the whole story makes an unfair judgment.

I don't know anyone else's bank account. I don't know where people spend their money. It's far too easy to sit in judgment without all the facts. You know it—you've listened to other people complain.

So it's no wonder that when your crisis hits, you're reluctant to let anyone know about it. Who wants to become fodder for the gossip mill? So you put up and shut up.

MONEY, MONEY, MONEY

Why is it that money brings out the worst in so many Christians? Why is it so easy to judge people without knowing all the facts?

It's because our entire lives are built around money: Our society runs on money, and people are often judged by how much money they have. We cannot live without money—it's the only way we get our food, keep our shelter, and obtain and run our vehicles. We work so we can get paid. Then we pay money so we can get to work. We pay taxes, we pay for college, we try to save for retirement.

Churches need money to pay workers, maintain buildings, pay utilities. The Bible teaches that pastors should be paid well enough that they don't have to worry about feeding their families or providing for the future. Missionaries need money to get to and stay on the mission field. Christian organizations need money so they can do their work.

There's no way around it—money is what runs life as we know it. Where people get into trouble is when they let money run them. People go to jail when they steal money, embezzle money, print their own money, or cheat on taxes in order to keep more money.

Money by itself is not a bad thing. Money is amoral—neither good nor bad. But it is powerful enough to bring out the worst in people. Everyone needs it; few people would say they have enough; most people want more. In God's hands, money can accomplish much for his kingdom. God doesn't *need* money to do his work, but he accepts the resources we offer for his kingdom. But what evil money can produce when it is in Satan's hands! He knows just how to use it to divide families, churches, and nations. He knows how to make it start wars. He knows how to make it ruin friendships. He knows how to keep Christians from even talking about it because they don't want to become casualties in gossip wars. How shameful when Christians let this happen.

If you've seen it in your church, no wonder you don't want to tell the people about your need. Perhaps you need a new church. Or maybe it's just a few people with big mouths. Maybe you need to be a catalyst to bring some perspective. Instead of grabbing onto tasty gossip, consider others' situations from their vantage point. You can be particularly sensitive to others right now because of what you're experiencing yourself. You need to be the one to say, "I don't think we can really judge that situation. We don't know all the facts." Or "Maybe there's something we don't understand here. Why don't we go talk to him about it and get the story straight?"

Even in the middle of your crisis, you can do others a great favor by being the one with the right perspective. You know from your crisis that you don't want people judging you for what they don't or can't understand. Apply that to others. Be the one to help break the power of money used or viewed wrongly in your Christian fellowship.

ASKING FOR HELP FROM THE CHURCH

The time may come when you are so desperate that you need to turn to someone for help. When your pride tries to stand in the way, remember two things:

- Perhaps God wants you to learn a lesson in humility.
- Perhaps God wants to let you see the body of Christ in action as it pulls together to help you.

Prayer support

Never take for granted the power of prayer. Never be ashamed to ask for prayer. Granted, there are those people who seem to always have crises, and you don't want to sound like that. But you won't, as long as you are sensitive to the situation. If you're in a small-group Bible study, for example, you can be more specific in your request for prayer than you would be in a more formal church-sharing session on Sunday night. In either situation, don't take a lot of time explaining the gory details of your crisis. Just state simply your need for God to intervene. If you continue to need prayer the next week, say so briefly. If and when an answer comes, be sure to report it with great praise to God and great thanks for the prayers of the fellowship.

I was involved in a wonderful women's Bible study for several months. I loved our small group, and the women really began to share their needs. After we'd been meeting for several weeks, my husband and I hit a financial crisis when a customer refused to pay for a very large job done in good faith. I asked for prayers that God would meet our needs and that we'd get more work to help pay the bills.

The response from those women was overwhelming. When I asked for prayer, I wasn't asking for their help, nor did I particularly want it. But these women weren't about to say "keep warm and well fed" and then go their merry way (James

2:15-16). No, they decided to do what they could to help us. One woman lined up several others to supply meals for us for a week. Others helped line up some work for us. Another friend in the group and her husband took us out to dinner for an evening away. Another wrote me a check for fifty dollars.

As much as my pride hurt, my self-esteem didn't hurt at all. As much as I cringed when grocery bags of food were brought to my house, I knew the women weren't looking down on me or gossiping behind my back. I knew that they really *wanted* to help. I could hold my head high and still accept help.

Financial support

That brings me to another way the church can help. If you can't feed your kids this week, don't let pride keep you from asking for help. Many churches have "care and share" funds. Often this fund is overseen by some leaders in the church, such as the deacons. When someone in the church has a need, he or she can ask for help and the fund is there. You only need to bring your request to the appropriate person.

You should not go to the church for help unless you are down to being unable to meet the basic needs—you can't feed your family this week. Most of your bills can be negotiated (as described in previous chapters), and your first resource ought to be your family if possible. But when you have no money for food, you're in trouble. The church wants to help you.

Does that send shivers up your spine? Would you rather chew nails than go to a group in the church and admit your need? If so, you're letting your pride get in the way. Besides, if those in charge of the fund do their job right, they will keep your request completely confidential.

You need not be ashamed. Remember these things:

The body of Christ wants to help you. In the original format of the church, everyone shared as each one was able. People willingly let go of their resources in order to help each other. That's why people put money into a care-and-share fund. No Christian wants to see another Christian's family go hungry— no matter what the cause.

You know your need is temporary. Those in charge of the fund will not give without discretion. They will weed out the man with the gambling problem or the people who would otherwise be a drain on the fund. The care-and-share fund is not meant to be anyone's source of income. Rather, it is meant to meet a temporary need. You know that you're not planning to come to them every week for the next year. God will provide, but this week, he may work through your church to provide.

You know that, when you can, you will pay it back so that others can be helped, as you were. You'll get back on your feet; you're reading this book so you can get through the tunnel. Don't worry about it right away, but be sure that when God's blessings come, you share them with the care-and-share fund. Repay when you can, as much as you can. That way, another person's needs can be met.

ASKING FOR HELP FROM THE GOVERNMENT

While I hope that your church can meet your immediate needs, you should not be ashamed to take advantage of other help if you find yourself in need for the long haul. The church cannot provide a regular income. If you've got desperate needs and if you qualify, you can get unemployment compensation, help from the local food pantry, and even welfare (which usually includes some form of food stamps and health care).

Don't get me wrong; I'm not an advocate of government help. It's clear today that too many welfare recipients are just living off the hard-earned money of people who work for a living. Our taxes are paying their meal ticket. Welfare was never intended to be someone's sole source of income for their entire life. Governor Tommy G. Thompson of Wisconsin explains his state's revamping of its welfare system by explaining, "It will make welfare what it was meant to be—a temporary hand up, not a permanent handout."[1] I believe that people who live their lives on welfare and food stamps have lost what this chapter is about—pride and self-esteem. They either have the attitude that the state is supposed to take care of them, or they simply have no sense of the self-esteem that comes from a job well done and a paycheck well earned.

But you need to realize that you're not in that category. Welfare was created for people like you: people who need a temporary hand up, as Governor Thompson said. I'm glad my taxes are able to help you on a longer term than my church gifts can help you. I'm glad food stamps and food pantries exist so your kids don't go hungry. I know that you see your need as temporary, that you're trying to get through the crisis the best way you know how, and that you'll eventually get off welfare.

If you have exhausted your resources and qualify for government aid, make use of available help. Hold your head high and keep your self-esteem intact. Accept the help while you need it, and actively seek to get off of welfare as soon as possible.

DOING WHAT IT TAKES

For most of us in a financial crisis, asking for help is taboo; going on welfare is a horrendous thought. Yet many would rather face either of those prospects than take a minimum-wage job. What would your friends think if they saw you bagging groceries or your wife flipping burgers at the local fast-food restaurant? Talk about your pride taking a beating!

Here's where you need to take a good hard look at yourself, your motives, and your pride. Here's where you let God take a double-edged sword and separate your pride from your self-esteem. Here's where you think about your true priorities.

This is also where you need to be creative. When you ask God for help and guidance, you need to be willing to receive it without letting pride get in the way. If a minimum-wage job keeps food on the table, then thank God for it!

You're in a crisis. What does that mean? I discovered an interesting definition in *Webster's* dictionary. Not only is a crisis a tragedy or upheaval, it is also defined as "a turning point, a condition of instability that leads to decisive change." In other words, a crisis forces decisions and changes that will make the situation better or worse. For Christians the question becomes, What do we need to do to follow the guidance God gives us? Then, beyond that, what does God want us to learn? The only way the crisis will get "better" is for us to let go of pride.

I can't say what direction that will take. I don't know what God might be teaching you—the possibilities are limitless. But I do know that pride will get in the way if you don't surrender it now.

- Will you let go of your pride?
- Will you allow God to go to work in your life?
- Will you willingly accept the guidance he gives?
- Will you do what it takes to get through your crisis?
- Will you set your priorities without pride influencing them?

Remember, crisis is not a permanent condition. It's a turning point. You're getting either better or worse. God wants to make the crisis work for you. Don't be ashamed of your crisis. Hold your head high, trust God for guidance, *follow that guidance,* and remember that somehow God is going to work all these things together for your good.

CHAPTER 7
PATIENCE
Why don't I get any miracles?

Never think that God's delays are God's denials.
Hold on; hold fast; hold out. Patience is genius.
COUNT DE BUFFON

You've heard the testimonies about how someone was on the verge of losing everything—then God supplied a job or cash or some other miracle just in time. You've heard the story about the missionaries who got just enough money right at the last minute.

You rejoice for such provision, but a nagging question remains: Why doesn't God do that for me? It's like you fell off the ship and the people on board shout down at you all the wonderful stories about how people have been saved from certain death in the ocean. The stories are great, but now *you* need to be saved! Why doesn't God do for you what he did for the others?

Well, the wonderfully profound answer is: I don't know. No one knows. We have examined in earlier chapters how God wants to work in your life to mold and shape you. The way he has chosen to do that in your life is different from the way he will work in another person's life. You'll run into trouble if you try to make comparisons.

"LORD, WHAT ABOUT HIM?"

Our Lord Jesus surrounded himself with twelve men. They were his provision for continuing his ministry after he left the earth. Unfortunately, these men often got into trouble arguing, not about theology, but about their places in the earthly kingdom they thought Jesus would set up.

Among the Twelve, Jesus had an "inner circle" of three—Peter, James, and John. These men accompanied him alone for some miracles as well as for the special revelation of the Transfiguration. Jesus singled out these men. He saw in them the qualities needed by the future leaders of his ministry on earth.

We know Peter denied Jesus, and Jesus reinstated Peter beside the Sea of Galilee. Jesus had great plans for Peter (who went on to become a strong leader in the Christian church in Jerusalem), but Jesus also warned him of future difficulty. Despite the fact that Peter's death would be tragic, Peter was told only to follow Christ.

But Peter turned and saw his friend John following them along the beach and asked, "Lord, what about him?" (John 21:21). Peter wanted to know what would happen to John. Jesus simply stated that whatever he wanted to do with John's life would happen, and it would be none of Peter's concern. "What is that to you?" asked Jesus. "You must follow me" (John 21:22).

Tradition tells that many years later, Peter was crucified for his faith—crucified upside down because he did not feel worthy to die as Jesus had died. John, on the other hand, lived to be very old. But he, too, was persecuted for his faith; he was exiled from his home to the island of Patmos. While there, he received the incredible revelation of the end times, recorded in the book of Revelation.

But there's more to the story. What happened to James, the

third person in the threesome (and, incidentally, John's brother)? Strange as it may seem, he was the first apostle to be martyred for the faith. Acts 12:1-2 explains that "King Herod arrested some who belonged to the church, intending to persecute them. He had James, the brother of John, put to death with the sword. . . . He proceeded to seize Peter also." The text goes on to explain Peter's miraculous escape from prison, as he was led by an angel through the prison gates and back to the home where the Christians were praying.

Why did James die while Peter was miraculously released? Why was Peter eventually subjected to a horrible death while John died of peaceful old age (albeit in exile)?

The answer, once again, is that no one knows.

Why does God allow one Christian organization to meet its financial need and another to flounder into bankruptcy? Why does God allow some missionaries enough to get to the field while others cannot raise enough support? Why does God answer my friend's financial need, but not send anything my way?

No one knows.

No one but God.

Peter tried to compare himself to John and got the only answer we will get if we compare our situation with others': "What is that to you?"

The bottom line is always the same: God is working to mold you into the person he wants you to be. His ultimate goal is to make you like his Son and to prepare you for life in his kingdom. What he needs to do in your life—spirit, attitudes, motives, relationships, past baggage, etc.—is different from what he needs to do in anyone else's life. How he chooses to work is entirely up to him.

So what do you do in the meantime? He told you that too: "You must follow me."

You are to learn to know him better. Don't allow your crisis to turn you away from God; rather, let it cause you to draw nearer. Diligently study the Bible to gain guidance for each day. Do what God tells you to do. Follow the guidance he gives—daily, hourly. Learn his lessons for you. Pray for protection, wisdom, and, yes, help. Trust that God will provide in his way, in his time. Know that whatever he does is with your best interest in mind.

How can you know that? How can you trust that much? Do you dare trust anyone that much?

Take a minute and think about the alternatives. Who would you rather trust with your life than God? You'd be in this crisis (or in another type of crisis) even if you had never chosen to follow him. Yet now, in the middle of your crisis, you know you have your Creator right there beside you. You're floundering in the ocean, and he is your life preserver. You're not just treading water throughout a crisis-filled life; you're saved from certain death and waiting for a glorious future! What could possibly be a better alternative? What better way to get through your crisis?

Let God work in your life. Let him work in your friend's life. And don't waste an ounce of energy comparing the two. *You must follow him.*

CONTENTMENT IN CRISIS?

What does it mean to follow Christ in the middle of your crisis? Before you can even get to that point, you need to learn a little secret. It's called *contentment.*

Now don't slam the book shut. I'm not going to tell you what you already know you should do but can't. I hesitate to even write about contentment because I know you have already heard the sermons about "being content in all things." I would probably have slugged anyone who advised me to "just be content" as we struggled through the worst parts of our crisis. Yet as I seek to encourage you, I cannot do so without including what I know (and you know) is the best medicine of all—being able to trust God so completely that you can truly rest in contentment. Contentment allows you to follow God as you paddle back toward the ship. It keeps you stroking, one arm over the other, trusting the Guide who leads the way.

But what does "contentment" mean? Should a Christian really be content during a crisis?

On the one hand, the answer is a resounding no. The very nature of a crisis is that it is a turning point. You don't *want* to stay in crisis; no one in his or her right mind wants to remain in a crisis. You want to move beyond it. Sometimes it takes a long time, but still you are moving past it.

On the other hand, the answer is also yes. You must discover a certain amount of contentment, even in the middle of the crisis. Otherwise you cannot get through the day-to-day grind. And it is contentment that gives you the willpower and clarity of mind to be able, eventually, to move beyond the crisis.

Contentment means that at the same time that you are accepting your situation, you're also seeking to move beyond it as God guides you. And through it all, you're learning what God has to teach you.

In a study of the book of Philippians, I came upon the following explanation of this well-known and often quoted verse: "I have learned to be content whatever the circumstances" (Philippians 4:11). What did Paul mean when he wrote of his contentment as he sat in prison? One commentator explained it like this:

[Paul] has *learned* the secret of deep peace based on detachment from his outward circumstances. In whatever conditions of life he finds himself, he discovers the will of God for his situation. This is not fatalism or indolent acquiescence which cuts the nerve of ambition or smothers endeavor. . . . It is, on the contrary, a detachment from anxious concern about the outward features of his life. This, in turn, arises from his concentration upon the really important things, the invisible and eternal (2 Corinthians 4:16-18) and, above all, upon the closeness of his fellowship with Christ on whose strength he constantly draws.[1]

Paul's experience of contentment is not out of reach for us. Why? Because Paul simply drew upon fellowship with Christ, something of which every Christian is assured. Contentment does not mean fatalistic acceptance of the junk that gets thrown your way. Instead, contentment is peace from deep within that allows you to keep your perspective, your self-esteem, your priorities, and your faith *in spite of* the junk. It allows you to keep moving in order to get beyond and above it.

Paul was not flippantly saying, "Oh, I'm content to sit here in prison." Not Paul! He probably burned with his desire to be out there traveling and preaching. Paul was not content in his situation; he was content *with God* in spite of his situation. He was content to do God's will right where he was. He wrote letters, talked to visitors, heard news from the churches, wrote more letters, and probably shared the gospel with his "captive" audience—the soldiers who were guarding him! Even during his second imprisonment, when Paul knew death was imminent, he asked Timothy to bring his scrolls and parchments (2 Timothy 4:13). Apparently Paul still had studying to do!

I would never say to you, "Just be content in your crisis." I know better because I know how hard it is, how much your mind whirls every moment around the financial worries, how you go to sleep restlessly and wake up worrying about what the new day will bring.

You and I both could use Paul's medicine—a big dose of contentment. Not that we are content to be in a financial crisis, but that we are content in spite of our financial crisis. Do you see the difference? When you have the contentment that comes from fellowship with Christ, you can keep your perspective, your self-esteem, your priorities, and your faith even on the worst days. You can trust God during the long swim back to the ship.

BUT IT'S JUST NOT FAIR!

You just get so tired of fighting it, don't you? You just want it all to stop so you can rest. You just want a break from the worry.

I know. I've been there. Some days I'm still there and I need to remind myself of the lessons I'm sharing with you.

One day, I learned an unexpected lesson from Joseph in the Old Testament. You remember the story—how he got sold into slavery by his jealous brothers, hauled off to faraway Egypt, sold to a powerful man named Potiphar, whom Joseph served well. Then Potiphar's wife came into the picture. She embarrassed herself in an attempt to seduce Joseph. She grabbed for his cloak and he took off, leaving the cloak behind. She took her embarrassment out on Joseph by falsely accusing *him* of attempting to seduce *her!* Potiphar, angry that his trusted servant had tried to take advantage of his wife, promptly had Joseph thrown into prison.

There Joseph sat. *What next, God?* Joseph may have wondered. *You brought me here to this foreign land; I did my best with what happened, but now I'm in prison under a false accusation. What do I do now?*

Let's think about this for a minute. Joseph was thrown into prison because of Potiphar's wife's lies. And from what we read in the Bible text, he was never vindicated. Who knows if Potiphar ever learned the truth? That would have really bothered me if I were Joseph. But God wasn't interested in that—God had big plans for Joseph. And the Bible tells us that God was with Joseph *in prison.*

> But while Joseph was there in the prison, the Lord was with him; he showed him kindness and granted him favor in the eyes of the prison warden. So the warden put Joseph in charge of all those held in the prison. . . . The warden paid no attention to anything under Joseph's care, because the Lord was with Joseph and gave him success in whatever he did. (Genesis 39:20-23)

Success? Now success, to me, would have meant clearing my name with Potiphar and being restored to my position as a trusted servant. But God let that story slip away as a new one unfolded in his preparation of Joseph for leadership in Egypt.

The lesson to me is that unfair things happen and we may *never* get justice—so what do we do?

The answer is key: We trust God and serve him as best we can right where we are.

Perhaps Joseph did try to obtain justice, as we can, but he was sprung from prison in an unexpected way—and not through Potiphar. Did he ever meet Potiphar or his wife on the street or in the hallways of the palace later in life? Does it really matter? What matters was that Joseph was true to his Lord and that the Lord was with Joseph.

Perhaps you've faced injustice. Lloyd and Karen certainly have. Injustice directly caused their crisis. What's their answer? They can attempt to obtain justice, but they must also realize that it may never happen. They should also trust that they might be "sprung" in unexpected ways. In the meantime, they can do what Joseph did. Do what they do best—continue to work hard at their business. They can operate with integrity even if they haven't been dealt with that way.

Perhaps you're facing discouragement as the crisis seems to have no end in sight, or the end is a long way off as you look at the bills and your feeble attempts to pay them. Once again, there's a lesson from Joseph. Do you know how long he was in prison under false accusation? Take a wild guess . . . then read Genesis 41:1. *Two years!* Joseph was in prison for two years! And he only got out at the whim of a pharaoh who needed to have a dream interpreted. Did Joseph languish in prison, whining and feeling sorry for himself? Nope. He worked hard for God and waited for God to work for him. He did what he did best and was given charge of the prison. All the while, God was preparing him for leadership beyond his wildest expectations!

The secret of patience is contentment. The secret of contentment is understanding that you are loved by God, that he is with you in your crisis, and that these trials "have come so that your faith—of greater worth than gold . . . may be proved genuine and may result in praise, glory and honor when Jesus Christ is revealed. . . . For you are receiving the goal of your faith, the salvation of your souls" (1 Peter 1:7, 9).

In the final analysis, it's the salvation of your soul that matters most—to you and to God. And in the meantime, you can remember that in this time of trouble, God is molding you for his kingdom. Do your best with the time God has given you, take advantage of God's blessings, learn his lessons, accept his molding, and look forward to eternity!

CHAPTER 8

PEACE
An island of peace in a sea of trouble

God takes life's broken pieces and gives us unbroken peace.
WILBERT DONALD GOUGH

I hope you've been able to find some encouragement thus far in the pages of this book. I wrote it for you, knowing how much pain you're feeling in the middle of your financial crisis.

This last chapter is about finding true and lasting peace. It's about not being on any more guilt trips, not beating yourself anymore.

Give yourself a break. Let go for a few minutes. Take some deep breaths.

- If the circumstances leading to your crisis were out of your control, realize that you just need to ride it out. Don't punish yourself for being in a difficult situation.
- If the pain is more than you can bear, remember that you don't need to bear it alone. Don't punish yourself with more pain and hurt. Give it to God, and let him carry your burdens.

- If it *was* your fault that you're in this crisis, don't punish yourself for making bad choices. In chapter 3 we talked about dealing with any sin that may have led you into financial crisis, and in chapters 4 and 5 we looked at specific ways to solve the immediate problem and keep it from happening again. Now that you are dealing with the root cause, repenting of sin, and acting to change, you can be free of guilt, be ready to move on, and find true and lasting peace.

I discovered two areas in particular that produce a lot of guilt among people in financial crisis, and I would like to briefly examine these. The first is the issue of dealing with bill collectors (who make you feel like you're the scum of the earth), and the second is the issue of tithing.

PAID TO HARASS YOU

There are the professionals who call from bill-collection agencies. There are the accountants from the companies to whom you owe money. There's the gas, electric, water, and phone companies who have the power to shut off vital resources.

What can you do to keep from being on a constant guilt trip and having no peace during your crisis as you deal with these people?

Avoid trying to explain your situation.

Unless the collector is someone who might care (such as an individual or someone from a small company where they know you personally), don't bother trying to explain your crisis. The people at the credit-card company didn't care that Sam lost his job, so it wasn't worth trying to tell them his sob story.

Remember, collectors are people paid to get a job done. They have no personal concern for you. Their computers dial the phone numbers for them, and they are paid to harass you into paying—that's it.

Don't get mad.

Those collectors are just people who, like you, are trying to make ends meet. Their job just happens to be to harass you. Chances are, if you met unknowingly at an exercise class, you'd get along just fine. They have nothing personal against you; if they quit their job tomorrow, they wouldn't care about your bill after that. Don't blame them for your problem— they didn't have anything to do with it. They're just in the middle. And the nasty notices on your bills are most often computer generated. Don't take them as an attack on your character.

Tell them you want to pay the bill and that you would like to work out payments.

You may be surprised to find that most people are willing to work with you. If you stay calm and reasonable, they will still be harsh, but they will work with you. They don't have a choice. But don't overextend yourself by offering more than you can afford per month. In the case of your utilities, you may have to go by their terms; then make it your goal to always stay on top of those bills while trying to conserve, lowering them as much as possible. In the case of credit cards, you want to try to pay above the minimum payments in order to stay ahead of the interest and actually pay down the balance. (See chapter 4 for more about credit cards.)

Keep good records of the agreements made.

After each conversation, record the outcome—and don't forget to get the name of the person to whom you spoke. You may need it later.

We once had to work out payments on our electric bill after

getting about three months behind. All along we kept thinking we could get caught up, but finally the dreaded shut-off notice appeared. My husband called and found out they had a set plan and an amount that had to be paid by the end of the week, with so much per week after that. We simply couldn't swing it and said so. We also explained that we were having difficult times, had three children in the house, and simply couldn't get by without electricity. So we made a counteroffer. This had to go up through two managers, but it was accepted. We agreed to pay a certain amount by the end of the month. The day after the payment was duly sent (to arrive in plenty of time before the month's end), our electricity was turned off while I was out for a walk with the children. Of course, I went into a rage. Luckily my husband stayed calm, called the electric company, and explained the agreement that had been made and whom we made it with (that's why it's good to keep track of names). The names made a difference—they knew we were for real. Within an hour, our electricity was back on.

The point is, offer to pay *something* every month. This keeps bill collectors at bay—if a payment (even a small one) shows up on the computer, your phone number probably won't be spit out to be called. If your local supplier sees you're making an attempt, he will be pleased.

One of my friends who has dealt with plenty of bill collectors takes the time to pray before calling collectors to talk about payments. She prays that they'll be sensitive, understanding, and willing to work with her.

Get an answering machine.
There comes a point when you've already talked to everyone, explained everything, and they just keep calling you because their computer keeps dialing your number. No one says you

have to keep talking to these people. On the days when you're feeling the worst, you can let the machine pick up the harassing calls. You can screen the calls and pick up those you want to answer. And don't feel guilty! This may help you keep your sanity.

Know your rights.
An article in *Business Week* explains that there are federal laws regarding how bill collectors can operate.[1] The Fair Debt Collections Practices Act gives rights to consumers regarding their collectors. Collectors cannot contact you at "unreasonable times or places" (very early in the morning or late at night, or at work if your employer disapproves). "As a protective measure, note when calls were made and what was said." If they cannot reach you, they may contact your family members or even your neighbors, but they cannot disclose the purpose of the call.

Within five days after contacting you, the collector must send a written notice stating how much is owed and who the creditor is. Unless the collector does so, it is barred from contacting you again. "Even if you do owe the money, the agency must stop contacting you if you write and tell it to do so. The agency may contact you again if a specific action is planned, such as filing a suit. Remember that collectors cannot falsely imply they are attorneys or government representatives or falsely suggest that you committed a crime." Many states also have their own debt-collection laws, so check with your state's attorney's office.

Just remember: Don't keep beating on yourself, and don't let anyone else do it. You're trying your best. At some point this *will* end. You *do* want to pay and fully intend to do so. Try to hold on to peace in the midst of this storm. You need it in order to keep from falling apart. Believe me, I know.

TO TITHE OR NOT TO TITHE

What about tithing during a financial crisis? Unfortunately, the wonderful privilege believers have of giving to their church and to other ministries has become a source of guilt, especially for those in financial crisis. People wonder:

- What should be my priorities when it comes to tithing during a financial crisis? Should I always give my tithe first, even if I can't pay other bills?
- What do I do about pledges I have made?
- Is this crisis a punishment because I haven't been giving enough to God?
- Can I expect God to help me out if I haven't been faithful to biblical principles?

Everything I've read and studied and heard about tithing has convinced me that it's a very personal issue. I cannot tell you what to do about tithing any more than I can tell you how to spend your money. But there are a few general principles and guidelines that I'd like to share with you.

What should be my priorities when it comes to tithing during a financial crisis? Should I always give my tithe first, even if I can't pay other bills?

I recently read about an issue concerning a church in Minnesota. It seems that a faithful couple, members of the church, had filed for bankruptcy. Now the U.S. Justice Department is involved, supporting one of the bankruptcy trustee's attempts to recover money by going after the church. They say that the money the couple gave to the church—even before they filed for bankruptcy—should have gone to the bill collectors. They want the church to cough up over $13,000 in tithes so creditors can be paid a portion of that money.

Whatever the eventual outcome, it is unfortunate that Christians have been called into account in this situation and that the court has any right to intervene.

But let's bring the situation closer to home. Suppose a church friend has owed you a hundred dollars for some time. This was not money you loaned; this is money owed to you, say, for services rendered. This person has never paid you, but regularly places large bills in the envelopes that go to the church's offering. You're glad for the gifts to the church, but you sure wish you could get what belongs to you. When we look at a debt situation from this perspective, we can see how giving money away while not paying debts is unfair to those to whom we owe money. If you were to act like the creditors in the case mentioned above, you would go to the church trustees and demand to be given the money from that person's offering envelopes until you were paid in full.

While I reserve judgment on the Minnesota case (I don't know all the details, and it involves a bankruptcy, which automatically gets the government involved anyway), it does seem that God would be honored, and a person's witness made more secure, if the debtor paid his or her debts first—whether these debts are within or apart from the church.

However, please understand that I am talking about a crisis situation only. We all have debts—I'm not saying pay off your house before you tithe! No, I'm saying that when you hit a crisis and get yourself in arrears with creditors, you must first work through the plan suggested in chapter 4. You must make arrangements with each creditor so that you're making payments monthly. You must not keep giving money to the church while at the same time *making no effort* to pay off your bills— God is not honored in that. Instead, try to work out a budget plan, tithe included, with the ability to keep each creditor happy. If you cannot come up with enough money to keep the creditors happy, you already know you have to cut back in some areas. If you've cut back as far as possible, then you must cut back on your giving for a time. Those past-due bills must be caught up. If you cannot give a tithe for a time in order to get yourself out of arrears (notice I said "out of arrears," not "out of debt"), then so be it. But don't get in the habit of using tithe money. You need to think of your tithe as a bill—only it's a bill with no bill collectors! In other words, you can use that money to get you out of the immediate crisis, but once you have a plan, you should go back to tithing. You might even want to "get out of arrears" with your tithe by catching up on what you couldn't pay.

When you hit a financial crisis, you need to put out the fires before you can assess the damage. If that means you need to use your tithe money, you must not feel guilty. It is not the unforgivable sin to use tithe money to get out of arrears; in fact, God is not honored by your giving money to him while forcing creditors to go unpaid. That is a bad witness for Christians and for the church.

Let's look at what Jesus said. Most Christians are surprised to discover that Jesus talked more about money than he did about any other single topic. On several occasions, Jesus spoke to the self-righteous Pharisees about giving, and always in a negative sense. The problem with the Pharisees was that they were giving with the wrong priorities and motives.

> "Woe to you, teachers of the law and Pharisees, you hypocrites! You give a tenth of your spices—mint, dill and cummin. But you have neglected the more important matters of the law—justice, mercy and faithfulness. You should have practiced the latter, without neglecting the former." (Matthew 23:23)

Jesus was clear that we ought to give, and that we ought to at least give a tenth (that is, tithe). But he also said that we are not to do that while forgetting other responsibilities—justice, mercy, and faithfulness. It seems that repayment of bills falls under any one of those categories. If you're in arrears, get current. Once you are current, continue to tithe to show your trust in God and your faith in him to meet your needs, and continue to keep your perspective on money—that is, it's all God's anyway. Then continue to faithfully work off your bills.

Remember that God doesn't *need* your money. God can accomplish everything he wants; it just so happens that he has chosen to do so through his body on earth, his people. Tithing should not become some legalistic command that causes you to count every penny so that you don't give a penny too much. Nor should it lead you to feeling guilty when you can't give everything you want to. Tithing was instituted for God's people so that they would always keep their money and possessions in perspective. It is the same for us today. It is proportional giving so that no one must give an unfair amount. It is money given so that we can help God's kingdom do its work in the world. In fact, if we refuse to give, God says we're actually robbing him (Malachi 3:8). He gives us 100 percent; if we refuse to give back a minimum of 10 percent, then it does amount to robbery! But in turn, God promises that if we are faithful in the foundational discipline of tithing, he will be faithful to meet all our needs (Malachi 3:10-12).

Some believe that tithing is not taught in the New Testament and that the concept is voluntary giving; that is, give all you can. Unfortunately, human nature doesn't hold well with that system. We can always find excuses to use God's money somewhere else. It helps to have a guideline (such as one-tenth) to give us the discipline to give. Many of us could give a lot more and live just fine. The tithe is not meant to be a ceiling in giving, but a floor. Christians ought never to turn away from a need by saying, "I already gave my tenth this month." God is not honored by that attitude.

A second problem with the Pharisees' giving was dealt with on another occasion:

> Jesus replied, "And why do you break the command of God for the sake of your tradition? For God said, 'Honor your father and mother' and 'Anyone who curses his father or mother must be put to death.' But you say that if a man says to his father or mother, 'Whatever help you might otherwise have received from me is a gift devoted to God,' he is not to 'honor his father' with it. Thus you nullify the word of God for the sake of your tradition." (Matthew 15:3-6)

Here Jesus was speaking of the practice of corban, a vow that could be taken requiring that person to dedicate money to God's temple that would otherwise have gone to support his aging father and mother. The Pharisees had become adept at dedicating money, using it for as long as they saw fit (it was dedicated, not given), and refusing to give it to their parents. Their large amounts of money dedicated to God's temple made them look very religious, but Jesus says this did not honor God because they were refusing to care for their own families. This action, in fact, nullified the very law the Pharisees claimed to uphold.

As an application in this day and age, it seems that God would require us to care for and feed our families. God is not honored by gifts given to the church while we don't care for the basic needs of our families or while we must go to others to meet our needs for us.

Please keep in mind that I'm always speaking here in terms

of a crisis. If you literally have to choose between putting money in the offering and putting any food on the table for your kids to eat, I'd suggest that God would tell you to feed your family. The point I'm making is don't feel guilty about caring for your family before giving a tithe. But be sure you're not making excuses—it can be easy to slip into that. Very seldom do people get to that desperate a strait—if your cupboards are completely bare, you need to buy some food. If you just want to eat out at McDonald's, then you're on the wrong track.

What do I do about pledges I have made?
A missionary friend recounted a story in which a young couple who supported them had a shortfall one month. They had enough money for one of three bills: the rent, the electricity, or their monthly pledge to the missionaries. They talked to the landlord who was willing to give them extra time; they called the electric company and were able to pay a minimum amount. So they sent their pledge off to the missionaries. They reasoned that they could work out the other payments and catch up, but "if we don't send our pledge, our missionaries may not eat."

I think these people are a great example in faithfulness. Yet realize that they were able to work it out first—and that's what I've suggested you do. Try to work it out so that you can keep up your pledges. If you need to make choices one month, seek God in prayer and in faith. If, like Sam, your income has dropped dramatically, then your one-tenth obviously drops, and you may need to adjust your pledges as well. However, you may choose not to do that and adjust your budget elsewhere. Your pledges should never be the first to go.

True, the poor widow gave all she had, but she was a widow (Mark 12:41-44). Her example shines because she chose to give all she had, she gave it without desire for notice, she gave it gladly, and she chose to then trust God to meet her needs. However, we can assume that she was older and had no children depending on her, and we can assume that she didn't owe all kinds of people money. Her example is not for all people to follow blindly—that wasn't Jesus' point. If you are alone in your crisis and choose to follow such an example in faith that God will meet your needs (and after you've taken care of your requirements for the month), then I praise your faith. And I'm sure God will meet your every need.

Is this crisis a punishment because I haven't been giving enough to God?

Are you in this crisis for not being faithful to the principle of tithing? Maybe; maybe not. But that shouldn't be your focus. True, God might be nudging you because you have not been giving as you ought. However, you might be in the crisis because you didn't follow other wise principles—such as spending only what you have, having the right perspective on money, avoiding putting your faith in a job or a future that is never certain. You might be in this crisis for one of those reasons and you were faithfully tithing the whole time! Maybe you didn't do anything wrong at all. Maybe you're in this crisis because God wants to use your faith and his faithfulness as an example. As he did with Job, God may have allowed your crisis to happen and will not explain why, but promises to show his love and power through it.

As you think about all you're learning from God in this, think about your attitude toward money. Ask God to help you see that all you have comes from his hand. Your goal is not merely to get out of this crisis and go back to the status quo. Your crisis ought to be showing you how little it takes to live comfortably, how faithful God is, how you ought to be responsible for what God has given by providing (but not hoarding) for the future, and how great it is to be able to give regularly to your fellowship as well as being able to help meet others' needs. Paul told the Corinthians:

Whoever sows sparingly will also reap sparingly, and whoever sows generously will also reap generously. Each man should give what he has decided in his heart to give, not reluctantly or under compulsion, for God loves a cheerful giver. And God is able to make all grace abound to you, so that in all things at all times, having all that you need, you will abound in every good work. . . . You will be made rich in every way so that you can be generous on every occasion. . . . This service that you perform is not only supplying the needs of God's people but is also overflowing in many expressions of thanks to God. (2 Corinthians 9:6-8, 11-12)

Giving is God's avenue to blessing. Out of your crisis should come a person willing to give and be "made rich in every way" so that you can give some more. Your giving results in others praising God for his provision. Soon you can be on the providing end of someone else's crisis. You can be money's master; it never again needs to master you. God is honored by faithful and cheerful giving. It shows your faith in him and helps him accomplish his work in the world.

Can I expect God to help me out if I haven't been faithful to biblical principles?
Yes, of course. That's like asking, "Will God save me if I've been sinful?" That's what salvation is all about! As we discussed in chapter 3, God wants to make you perfect, he wants you to grow closer to him, and he wants you to be faithful to

him in all areas of your life. Money is one of the most difficult areas. God wants you to get out of your crisis. In the meantime, he wants you to learn the lessons he is teaching you through this crisis. Then you must be faithful and responsible with what he has given you and with the lessons you have learned.

"PEACE I LEAVE WITH YOU"

Our Lord Jesus, facing the cross, left these wonderful words of comfort with his disciples: "Peace I leave with you; my peace I give you. I do not give to you as the world gives. Do not let your hearts be troubled and do not be afraid" (John 14:27).

The peace Jesus promised to his followers obviously was not absence of conflict—the early believers faced conflict from all sides. Instead, it meant a deep inner peace made possible by the presence of the Holy Spirit in each believer's life. The Holy Spirit's peace allows us to find, deep within, a peace from God as we face the storms and stresses of life. This isn't peace as the world gives or as we might want it to be. It isn't a promise of life without problems. Instead, it is peace in spite of the problems, the stresses, the crises.

The apostle Paul wrote: "Do not be anxious about anything, but in everything, by prayer and petition, with thanksgiving, present your requests to God. And the peace of God, which transcends all understanding, will guard your hearts and your minds in Christ Jesus" (Philippians 4:6-7).

Paul explained that as we face the storms and stresses, we can turn our worries into prayers and present our needs to God. And you know what will happen? You'll experience God's peace. Your heart and mind will be blanketed with it—guarded against any unwanted intruders. Your stomach will stop churning. You'll be able to sleep. You'll be able to face the day without tears. You'll be able to focus on what needs to be done.

You'll be able to deal with your kids without yelling at them. You'll be able to get through the crisis intact.

How can that be? The conflict is still there; we still have a long way to go to get out of this crisis. The peace comes not from feeling good about our situation. It comes from knowing the one truth that matters most: *God is in control.* That alone is the foundation of our peace. No matter what happens, we can trust our God to be at work for us.

We can make it. The journey may be long ahead of us, the light at the end of the tunnel not yet visible. But God is here with us. Place your hand in his and walk forward with him, unafraid, unharried, and at peace.

NOTES

Chapter 3: Prayer
1. James Boice, "Responding to God in Prayer," in *Practical Christianity* (Wheaton, Ill.: Tyndale House, 1987), 415.
2. Warren Wiersbe, *Why Us? When Bad Things Happen to God's People* (Old Tappan, N.J.: Fleming H. Revell, 1984), 104–113.
3. Ibid., 109.
4. Ibid., 111.

Chapter 4: Plan
1. Howard L. Dayton, "How to Get Out of Debt," in *Husbands and Wives* (Wheaton, Ill.: Victor Books, 1988), 415.
2. Margaret Mannix, "How to Bail Out of Debt," *U.S. News and World Report,* 15 February 1993, 83.

Chapter 6: Pride
1. Candy Berkebile, "The State of Welfare," *Family Voice,* June 1994, 13.

Chapter 7: Patience
1. Ralph P. Martin, *Philippians,* Tyndale New Testament Commentaries (Grand Rapids: Eerdmans, 1988), 177.

Chapter 8: Peace
1. Suzanne Woolley, "Beware, Bully-Boy Bill Collectors," *Business Week,* 16 November 1992, 98–99.

INDEX

A

answering machine *102*
anxiety. *See* worry

B

balanced life *75*
bankruptcy *57*
bill collectors *100, 102*
bills
  categorizing *42*
  prioritizing *42, 45*
blame *12, 101, 113*
budget *12, 45, 74*
Burkett, Larry *42*

C

Christmas gifts *55*
church
  asking for help from *83-84*
comparisons *79, 89*
contentment *92, 94, 97*
counseling *12*
  financial *56*
credit cards *57, 74, 101*
creditors *49, 56, 58, 105*
crisis *9, 19, 110*
  definition of *6, 87*
  getting a handle on *42*

D

David, king of Israel *26*
debit cards *54*
depression *78*
discouragement *97*

E

Elijah *36*

F

family
  communication *70, 73*
  enlisting help of *56, 73*
fault. *See* blame
filing system *42*
food *66, 84, 109, 113*

G

God
  answers prayer *23, 27-28*
  blaming God *14*
  his goals for us *14, 17, 29, 79,*
    87, 91
  personal relationship with *22, 78*
  questioning God *7*
government
  asking for help from *85*
groceries. *See* food
guilt *6, 14, 26, 40, 99, 107*

H

Hannah *27*
Hezekiah, king of Judah *24*

J

James, apostle 635 *90*
Jesus
  teaching about money *106, 108*
Job, book of *61, 75*
John, apostle *90*
Joseph *95*

judging others   *79, 82*
justice/injustice   *96, 106*

L
loans   *56-57*
lottery   *16, 28*

M
miscellaneous expenses   *44, 69*
money
    "mad money"   *12*
    becoming your master   *16, 111*
    importance of   *15, 81*
    power of   *16, 82*
    sharing needs with others   *79*
    what the Bible says about   *63,*
        65, 81, 106, 108

N
National Foundation for Consumer
    Credit   *56*

P
Paul, apostle   *16, 30, 32, 93, 112*
Peter, apostle   *90*
pledges   *104, 109*
prayer
    about money   *8, 21, 29, 32, 39*
    approaches to   *17, 23, 26, 30*

barriers to   *34*
types of   *11*
when God doesn't seem to hear
        10, 17, 33, 36
yes, no, wait answers   *28-29*

R
repentance   *34*

S
savings   *75*
self-esteem   *6, 77, 86, 95*
sin   *14, 34*
spouse
    and money problems   *12*
    date night with   *70*

T
team effort   *13*
tithing   *104, 106-107*
transportation   *69*

U
utilities   *69, 100-101*

W
welfare   *85*
Wiersbe, Warren   *29-30*
worry   *7, 17, 40, 95, 112, 113*